Cambridge University Press
Fetter Lane, London

Bombay, Calcutta, Madras
Toronto

Macmillan

Tokyo

Maruzen Company, Ltd

Copyrighted in the United
States of America by the
Macmillan Company

THE WORLD
of the
NEW TESTAMENT

THE WORLD
of the
NEW TESTAMENT

By
T. R. GLOVER

CAMBRIDGE
AT THE
UNIVERSITY PRESS
1931

To

DIL & ELEANOR CALVIN

Haud equidem sine mente reor sine numine divom
Adsumus et portus delati intramus amicos

CONTENTS

PREFACE

The suggestion was made to me some time ago by a friend well known in the world of education that a book was needed which would let the ordinary student of the New Testament realize something of the society in which the Early Church found itself, something of the ideas and hopes and the traditions on which men lived, something of the political conditions which had made the Roman Empire and which still sustained it, something of the everyday life of the ordinary people in street and home. It is to meet that suggestion that this book has been written. In such an attempt as this the two chief difficulties are to omit and to interpret. Others would have laid stress on other facts and other phases of the world here described, and would be justified in their choice. That is one reason why the period is so amazingly interesting. "Here is God's plenty", as Dryden said of Chaucer. For those who wish to go farther there is added at the end of the volume a short list of books that will really take them into the subject—generally books which will be found enjoyable.

T. R. G.

CAMBRIDGE

27 February 1931

I

INTRODUCTION

In the New Testament we have the opening pages of a story, familiar to us, but yet very insufficiently realized. The story is two-fold; it shows us a new conception of life in an old world, and at the same time a new society within an older and a much greater society. In that world, and that society, the books of the New Testament were written. The writers did not need to paint the picture of that old world for their first readers. It is from other sources that we have to draw our knowledge of their environment. From those sources we realize that it was a world of great ideals, a world of very great achievement in every phase of man's life, in social life, in political and national life, yes, and in the higher and more universal life which touches such things as exploration, geography, astronomy and all other branches of science and art, of philosophy and literature. That is the background; and one of the fascinating things in New Testament study is the problem of the influence of this great world upon the new conception of life; they will react upon each other, that is inevitable, but which will be the more potent? Will the new conception of life hold its own, or will it be so modified as to lose its value and its force?

In the next place there is the story of the new society within the much greater society of the whole Mediterranean world. The one is a mere group, a group inspired with new principles and new convictions, possessed of a new objective, all related to the central conception of a new type of life altogether, a life in a new relation to God but to God conceived in a wholly new way. Yet the group is very far from understanding in its fulness the conception for which it stands; it does not yet realize what is implied in its new relation to God. The interpretation of God is always difficult, and in this case the difficulty is not lessened by the greatness and profundity of the conception. The story is one of conflict, of course; and to conquer that old world the new society must be equal to facing the intellectual standards, and to meeting the needs that are implied in the thought-out society, that underlie it and animate it. There are in every society only too many of the unthinking and the unintelligent; but a new conception of life, if it is to conquer the world, has to win the thinking and the intelligent, and it has to satisfy them at their best and at their highest. Not only have their intellectual conceptions to be faced, whether to be reconciled or to be overcome, but their artistic instincts and their imagination have to be satisfied; and in the background there is always their pride in the tradition of the greatly better days of the past. It may be possible for the new society with its new conceptions to achieve all this; or it may be that the old world finds in the new group something else, something that will meet yet greater spiritual needs which it feels, and meet them with a compensating power of such force and value as to outweigh any failure in the other directions.

The new society has yet to think out its new principles for itself. It has to understand what these new principles mean in relation to the ordinary facts of experience, to physical life, and again in relation to the traditions and the inheritance of the larger society that is round about it, that overshadows it. It has to think out its new principles in relation to the whole intellectual life of that larger society. It has to grapple, for example, with the very idea of thinking which possesses that larger society. Standards of thinking and habits of thinking do not uniformly prevail in all races or at all periods; but that great Mediterranean world was fundamentally intellectual, as a result of six centuries of the keenest activity of the best minds which perhaps the world has ever seen. Greek culture, the essence of which was the habit of facing and testing ideas, was all round the Christian group; and the group had to face a world of thought, to face the conclusions which the world drew from this thinking, the dogmas which the generations had achieved and handed down as the foundations of all speculation and of all life.

Yet again, the new principles have to be re-thought in relation to the whole social, imperial, and economic fabric of the world round about. That old world had had too much of war and waste, the sheer destruction of human life, the loss of home and gear and all that makes life livable. Very generally it had lost heart and hope; it had ceased to believe in anything but blank endurance, but acceptance of whatever the selfishness of rulers and adventurers and the malice of irrational fortune might bring upon them. There is an avowed scepticism and there is an unavowed scepticism which may influence society; both are to be found in

3

that ancient world. It had in a sense ceased to believe in the old ideals of freedom which once informed the social life and the thinking life, even while it cherished them. It was still easier to lose faith in the new monarchies, Greek or Roman, in the restorations and reformations of the social order. Sheer Chance had been too much and too evidently the dominating power, the goddess of all the world. The world despaired on the whole of reaching truth, though it still felt what the philosophers had urged for centuries —that man was born to examine life, and must and will examine it; yet all the examination seemed somehow inconclusive; the experts differed so much and yet came short of their goal.

So men fell back upon the compromise of accepting while they rejected what the experts told them; all eclectics, as Novalis said, are sceptics, and the more eclectic the more sceptical. The world was weary of ideas; a person who cross-examined men as Socrates did is unthinkable in our period; and yet to be weary of ideas and to despair of truth is to be conscious of both, it is a tacit admission that thought and truth are essential. Weary of the philosophers, mankind is even more weary of the personal ambitions of politicians and of kings; it has turned to the practical business of life, to that sordid poverty-stricken notion which to-day the unreflective call "getting on with the job". It generally means the job of physical living, of escaping thought; here it also meant the job of administering the Empire, of keeping roads in repair, of looking after the food supply, of collecting the taxes, and providing some sort of law and order.

INTRODUCTION

The world is immensely set and fixed in all its ideas and inhibitions, philosophic and economic; nothing can ever be changed; men have seen all that can be devised.[1] Yet with all its disillusionment the world was still cherishing its splendid past, its last idealism. The past had been great, there had been an age of genius, and against that great past the world measured all that was presented to it. Unequal to our ancestors, sorely declined as we may be, we feel that the new heroes and the new ideals presented to us must measure up, not so much against ourselves, as against the great whom we remember, whom we idealize. "Let us remember", says Aristotle, "that we should not disregard the experience of ages"; and he adds, "Sometimes men do not use the knowledge they have".[2] The Graeco-Roman world is all for keeping the heritage of the ages, but not for venturing upon too abrupt a use of it.

Our story is one of conflict. Will it be victory for the new or for the old, or will it be, as commonly in human affairs, compromise? Let us glance for a moment at the experience of modern missions, whether among the savages on the Congo River or among the civilized in India. A thoughtful man does not work long among people of either kind before in ceaseless succession new and difficult questions present themselves. How far is the advocate of the new faith to recognize the social and economic traditions of the people among whom he lives? For instance, in the history of mankind it has

[1] Cf. Marcus Aurelius xi, 1, 2, the man of forty, if he has any sense, has in a way seen all that has been or will be.
[2] *Politics*, ii, 5, 16.

5

long been a difficulty to determine the frontiers of
magic and medicine. Perhaps it is not yet decided,
even among civilized people, that the two things are
distinct; popular ideas of suggestion keep open a broad
No-Man's-Land between the two spheres. Is the traditional treatment of smallpox, for example, in
southern India, by killing a hen and pouring its blood
over an image or a lump of mud, magic or medicine?
If it is magic, is the magic also idolatry? May a
Christian use such a prescription? This is an actual
case which has occurred. Is astrology compatible with
Christian faith? What does the Gospel say to poly-
gamy? It has in some places seemed to offer a great
opportunity for shrewd polygamists, who were tired of
unnecessary and middle-aged wives; and the missionary has had to decide whether the unnecessary
wives were to be ruined by the polygamous husband's
acceptance of Christ. How many centuries did it take
for the Christian world to decide whether slavery is
economically right, and whether what is morally
wrong can be economically right? When we see an
independent native church in India and in China, we
shall see a great deal of Indian and Chinese philosophy
incorporated in Christian thinking, which will certainly
be uncongenial to ourselves, but which may or may
not be germane to the mind of Christ. How much of
religious usage is to be preserved with or without a new
significance, transformed and assimilated? Or is all
ritual of the older religion rejected, as a danger to the
new faith? In the phrase of the parables, how far is
it wise to go in putting new wine in old wineskins?

How far could the adherents of the new Christian

faith in that old Mediterranean world go in accepting the ordinary education of the day? Was it too pagan? Was it inevitable unbelief and idolatry? Is style in this instance to be dissevered from thought, or can the Christian accept the great literary traditions of the past untouched by their paganism? Could he accept the art of the past? That meant the statues, the idols, the Aphrodites, the temples; if he rejects these, what could art mean? But if art is rejected, the life of man is mutilated; and was it conceivable that life in Christ lacked something that life without Him gave? I was criticized myself in southern India for speaking to Christians of the great temple of Madura as an architectural achievement; it is carved all over with idols; it has heathenism in every stone; supposing the whole community become Christian, what can it do with a temple whose every stone defies Christ, to say nothing of decency?

Once again, how far could the adherents of the new Christian faith go in accepting the economic order of existing society? Here we have to remark that there is, in the main, less question, because in most ages of our history the economic challenge is never so explicit as the literary; economic thinkers, and still more, business people who do not think, seem to resent contradiction more than artists, philosophers, or men of letters; we accept the economic rules of everyday life, we are slow to recognize economic facts, even when they clash with what otherwise we believe. How far could the social and personal habits of the day be accepted? What is moral, what is immoral? The usages of daily life, like the Imperial order which crowned the whole structure of society, were all tainted with idolatry. The problem of the supremacy of the State, the problem of standardization by social environment and common education,—perhaps even to-day we do not find it easy to solve these.

The church, as we see, was face to face with a thought-out society; its own principles were not yet thought out; and the question the student soon reaches is this: How far were those early Christians conscious of a unity of experience, a unity of ideal, with that larger society, how far conscious of diversity, and how far was the diversity significant or material? Must all life be remodelled—and why? Or only some of it? All the old familiar problems of drawing lines, of the number of grains that make a heap, etc., are revived; endless distinctions have to be drawn with every kind of uncertainty; and as the watcher of the struggle realizes what is going on, and how vital are the issues for all time, the fascination of the study grows. It is part, after all, of our own story, this conflict between the ideals of Christ and the traditions of our race.

It may seem a simple division of society to distinguish in it the three groups, the worst, the neutral, and the best; but simple as the division may seem, it is a question where in that ancient world the war was really waged. There is in every human society a large mass of decent or half-decent people, either quite un-reflective, or only reluctantly stirred to occasional reflection. I cannot help asking myself whether in the ancient world that mass of unreflective mankind was not, as it so often is, a sort of body of Patroclus, almost dead in itself, for which the contending forces were battling. From time to time this neutral section woke to some consciousness and realized dimly that something was happening, felt vaguely that some change was inevitable, and wondered whether the change need be so great after all. Each successive awakening has been apt to mean some progress recorded; but the progress is always slow, and hard to track through a maze of compromise. Putting all this section of society on one side, we have to ask whether the real conflict of the church was with the best or with the worst. Would the best elements co-operate with the church in relation to the world? The classical scholar will hesitate to affirm this. But if the best of society are to co-operate with the church, the best have to be won. It is the thesis of this book that the best was very good indeed, and that it was won for Christ.

There are two lines of approach. As in modern India the capture of the untouchables by the Christian church, sometimes a whole tribe at a time, is recognized by thoughtful Hindus as one of the greatest challenges and dangers to their religion, so in the ancient world we find the Christian apologist pointing with something of pride to a new life in the depraved, to manhood and womanhood remade in a larger mould, a truer and more God-like. Secondly, there is the appeal to the best elements in the world along the lines of agreement.

Then for what are we to look in our study of this ancient world? There are various choices. We may, if we choose, look at the worst—at the moral degradation of society. We may steep our minds, if we

have nothing better to do, in Juvenal, or perhaps
Martial, and recall heathen ways and habits, which,
it might be said, may be found again almost as easily
in Paris or New York; or we may study certain recognized practices of society and the judgments of human
nature and morals which underlie them, practices and
judgments with which the Christian apologist challenged his heathen critic. Or we can turn, as so many
do to-day, to the emotional movements in society, and
study the mystery religions. Perhaps it would be a
good thing to study the mystery religions, for to-day
they are brought before us with an enthusiasm that
outruns knowledge. The different cults are recklessly
blended to produce a general type. But it is far from
clear that the type which modern writers offer us ever
existed. We do not know exactly what was taught in
one or another of these religions; where we are given
hints, it is not always clear what those hints imply; the
modern advocates of the mystery religions seem careless in this matter, and in any case they are not dealing
with theologies which have been thought out as the
Christian theology has been. We may be too easily the
victims of casual similarities or loose analogies; and
some of the most assured writers on the subject can
hardly be acquitted of guess-work. It is very difficult
to date the documents on which we have to depend for
our inside information; we do not know at all precisely
the range of diffusion of these cults nor the extent of
their popularity; they may have been essentially secret
and esoteric; but perhaps the most important fact is
the small attention which the apologists give to the
mystery religions as compared with the great tradi-

tional worship of the Olympians. The apologists were less interested in the mysteries than some of our contemporaries, and it is not always safe to flatter ourselves that we have got beyond the outlook of the ancients. Certain modern scholars, for instance, have discovered truths about the Pharisees which Jesus missed; and it is indeed something of a triumph for the reader of forgotten books to recognize character and to see spiritual issues more clearly than Jesus.

In this book I propose, in the main, to look beyond Juvenal and the mysteries to the great outstanding types of Greek and Roman which would in that day have been accepted as mankind's best, to study the highest achievements in character and the thought-out life, and not altogether to forget the average man. What we find at last is that Christ has conquered the ancient world, and the question is how that victory was won. The ancient world produced, as I have said, great types of men, and we miss something of the victory of Christ if we fail to realize the grandeur of the types which he captured.

But two questions of import are raised. What was it that won the victory of the Christian church? Was it the organization? That is one view which remains in the mind from the famous fifteenth chapter of Gibbon. But another view is suggested by Wilamowitz which has surely more depth; for an organization, if it is to capture a man or a society, must have some central idea. Wilamowitz says that the Christian religion overcame the competing religions because it had most effectively hellenized itself. The suggestion may seem strange, but when its real meaning is made clear it becomes very attractive. What he means, I think, is this, that of all the faiths in the ancient world the Christian religion in the long run was the most conceivable to a deeply reflective nature; it was the most germane, the most possible, for the best thinking of that ancient world; it cut out, once and for all, every compromise with those elements of religion which the clearest minds and the purest natures recognized to be weak or wrong, and it kept and reinforced the sublimest teaching of the great philosophers and the instincts of the purest hearts; and further it made all available for ordinary people in a way beyond the dream of the old philosophers; in short, of all religions it was the most congenial to the thought-out life. Whether this be the precise meaning of Wilamowitz, or whether I have developed it, as is possible, in a way that he might not endorse, the suggestion is of high value, for in any case it prompts to a closer study of the relations between the Gospel and the best thought of the ancient world along lines which are far from exhausted.

But, we are bluntly asked, how far was it victory at all? A French writer, Remy de Gourmont, commends Catholicism to us because, he says frankly, it is "Christianity paganized". The view is somewhat widely held by modern apologists for medieval religion in some of its surviving forms that there are certain permanent elements in the human mind, certain types of idea necessary to human thinking, which, though definitely ignored or rejected by Christ, are likely to prove stronger, and to appeal to men, and especially women, more vividly, than the pure and reformed faith to which he limited himself. Jesus, at this rate, failed; the outcome was a compromise in favour of what he died to abolish. But, whether it was victory or not for the church in the days of Constantine, or by the days of Luther or Loyola, whether the victory be yet to come, this much at least is true; a place was made for the ideas of Jesus, and very often that is enough. He himself, at all events, in his parables suggests, and history seems to confirm him, that his ideas fertilize themselves, and that once lodged, they grow and are fruitful, bringing forth an hundred-fold. Whatever compromises the church may have made, a new note was struck in morals; a new conception of God was offered to mankind. Jesus himself began to become familiar to the heart of man; and eventually —a very long eventually it was—there was more and more room made for Jesus Christ and his ideas, though we have to wait for the Renaissance and the Reformation to see the outcome; and the future has still developments to reveal.

Yet another criticism is suggested. Is it not arguable that those great types of antiquity which we propose to study were not won at all, but simply disappeared from society, were in fact lost, with much else? To that my answer is this. I turn to Euripides' play, the *Hippolytus* (388), and there I find Phaedra speaking. She is the heroine of the play, a mere woman, but a Greek woman, though, perhaps, like the heroines of Euripides, more reflective than Greek women commonly were. She has been thinking things out, she says, and "When once I saw the truth, there was no drug that I could take to unsee it and lose again what once I had seen". In Gilbert Murray's translation:

> This is the truth I saw then, and see still;
> Nor is there any magic that can stain
> That white truth for me, or make me blind again.

There, in a sentence, we have the essential Greek habit of mind; and I submit that it did not disappear. There came a dramatic moment in the Council of Nicaea, when a formula was on the verge of being accepted, which would have reunited Christendom, or at least would have cloaked and concealed a deep cleavage, and one man, a Greek from Egypt, stood up, with the awful clarity of Phaedra, and asked the assembly whether they meant one thing or the opposite. He saw the issue; he insisted on clear Greek thinking; the assembly grasped the issue, and an epoch-making victory was won for a definite conception of Christ's nature. The late J. B. Bury said that the victory of Arius would have meant the premature disappearance of Christianity—a delicate concession for such a rationalist, but a confirmation of the clarity of Athanasius. But one has only to live with such men as Justin and Clement, and even the Tertullian, whom I am almost alone in loving—Tertullian clear as a Stoic on Nature and on first principles—to realize that the Greek habit of mind was not lost; Christianity and Hellenism belonged to each other. Dean Inge says very much the same thing when he calls Christianity the least oriental of the great religions.

If then we find that the new religion, the new inspiration, the new society, was accepted by some of the best minds in the ancient world, why was it? The challenge is a great one. Why was it? What was it in that new religion that won the best thinking of the world? Of course we have to admit that, whatever it was, side by side with it we find the influence of Roman bureaucracy, of the Successors of Alexander, of the civil servants and lawyers of Rome, with all of whom we shall have to deal. But it is more significant that the new religion heightened the old Greek emphasis on the value of the individual, and of the individual mind, and reinforced Plato's teaching upon the necessity of clear and true thinking about God. What is the Christian Gospel in the long run but a more glorious statement of Plato's sentence that we must, in all cases, see and tell the truth about God? If the new society borrowed, as we all do, from contemporary methods of organization, if the organization was wrong in that it overdid its proved effectiveness, this is a challenge to us to study the Roman mind. But the apologists make it clear how very Greek the Gospel is—the beautiful, they tell us, belongs to Christ wherever it is; if the law was the schoolmaster to bring the Hebrew to Christ, the Greek's schoolmaster was philosophy, and led him in no other direction. There is many a page in Clement, of which it is difficult to say whether it owes more to Christ or to Greek literature, until you realize that there is no contradiction between them, that they harmonize in real beauty. There is much truth in the suggestion that the mind of Christ and his ideas never found their perfect expression till they were given in Greek.

Our object in these chapters is to see the world in which the new society found itself. But, when we look for the world, it is so obvious that we are apt to miss it. What is it that makes the world, our environment, the conditions of our thinking, our own minds, anywhere or at any time? For example, to explain the English to the Chinese or the Americans, or any other foreigners, where should one begin? How should one explain the unspoken and the unformulated axioms which underlie all our thinking? Even those of us who, strangely different from the Gael, are unconscious of our grandfathers, are made by our grandfathers, our own and other people's. To explain the English, surely Hengist and Horsa must come into the story as well as Queen Victoria. Surely William the Conqueror, Henry the Eighth, Cromwell and Robert Walpole, had in their different ways something to do with the making of the English mind. Could we omit Shakespeare, or William Tyndale, who translated the New Testament for the first time from the Greek, Dr Johnson and Sir Joshua Reynolds, or even Sir William Jenner? Something would have to be said about the soil and the crops, the landscape, the fog, and the sea. What are the factors that make us? From how far back do they come? We are made, above all, by memory and belief, by memory of events, traditions, legends— but most of all by belief. We are made by economic usage, by economic facts and laws, by economic fancies, by sheer habit and convention; and belief underlies them all, and makes us. We are made by all that touches our spiritual nature, by art, by ballad and story, religion, perhaps science—again, belief, belief, belief. We are made by the sense of nationality, which is belief again—by all sorts of cross-influences, from enemies, traders and travellers; war, curiosity, fashion, all contribute; the philosophy, the art and the literature of the foreigner come in; and all becomes a unity, interpreted somehow and harmonized in belief.

It is thus that we have to study the ancient world; and I would claim for our study that it is not mere archaeology or antiquarianism; it is a real inquiry into the mind and life of man, a training for ourselves. It is the study of a thought-out society, as I have kept saying, at its best, of a civilized world with a great education and a splendid past, a world with a literature, a philosophy, a history, an art, a spiritual ancestry, familiar and beloved for centuries, a world with postulates, the axioms and inhibitions that make man, a world made one by the Mediterranean, by the climate, by the universal growth of the olive, by the spread of the two languages—or three, if we may reckon Syriac—by the common culture based on belief, by the common government which brought peace to mankind with clear conceptions of law and justice never yet lost. This is the world that the early church had to win, and the grandeur of its task and the greatness of its victory give us the measure of its powers. "I came not to destroy but to develop" is a sentence that has proved true.

THE GREEK

There can be few things more moving than to stand on the Acropolis of Athens with the Parthenon behind you, and to look down on that strange little mound, on which the Apostle Paul, to the amusement of his listeners, explained an absurd new religion from somewhere in the East, which he seemed to suppose was to dominate the life, the religion, the thought and the culture of Hellas, the symbol of which was the Parthenon towering on high before his hearers. Could ever a man have had a more overpowering background? The merest glance upward told every listener of the absurdity of the speaker; his refutation was the beauty of that unexampled temple which had stood there for five hundred years, every stone of it (so Plutarch said) as fresh as if yesterday from the hand of the carver. There the Parthenon still stands, and still speaks of the race that made it, that thought it first and then made it, hand and brain paired for once in human story. For us the Parthenon means more than the goddess to whom it is consecrated; it is a symbol of the Greek mind.

The work of the Greek is, above all things, the discovery of the individual. To him, as a modern scholar has put it,[1] the chief curse of barbarism was that it swamped the individual; it took from him that freedom, that initiative, in thought and act, that makes

[1] J. A. K. Thomson, *Greek and Barbarian*, p. 60.

a character. It is as difficult to name a date for the emergence of the Greek race as it would be in the case of the English. The hero in Homer is already as individual as the fellow-citizen of Pericles. But the poets are all for the individual. What else is the meaning of Pindar's insistence on native genius as opposed to instruction, on the born poet as distinguished from the products of the schools?[1] It was Solon who discovered, and expressed in emancipating laws his discovery, that the great asset of Athens is the Athenian citizen, who looks at the world for himself, studies the sea, understands commerce, and sails his own ship; let him be free to use his intelligence as he shall choose, and Athens shall have the power and the glory. That discovery made a new Athens, the world's most valued city. It throbs through the great speech of Pericles. The individual citizen is Pericles' theme, with his power of judgment, and the immense gain to the state when the individual brings that power of his to bear on everything that can be presented to him in a society—law, battle, navigation, or beauty in all its manifestations of pageant, music, letters, and architecture. No doubt, as Simonides says in a famous fragment, "the city trains the man"; but the city had as yet no organization for teaching the young. What was the irony of Plato was the history of the generation before him; Anytos, the absurd enemy of Socrates, was historically right; the individual Athenian picked up his education from his father, his father's friends, the city. All was fluid, and far from ineffective. Plato had

[1] Pindar, *Olymp.* 2, 86; 9, 100. Compare Phemios in the *Odyssey*, xxii, 347, self-taught and inspired by God.

other ideas; and after him Aristotle discusses the question of state control of education. In the great days it was not yet organized, and it is worth noting that the organization of education and the decline of genius, by chance or of necessity, came to Athens together. We must remember the surprise of Herodotus at finding exclusive castes in Egypt, at realizing the reluctance of the Egyptians to borrow ideas, and the results of it in a society possessed, no doubt, of ancient learning and ancient arts, interesting in all its contrasts with a later-developing Greece, but stereotyped, bound fast to rule and tradition, secure against further developments. He remarked the same antipathy to change in the barbarous Scythian, a curious parallel between civilized and savage. The historian's surprise is evidence of another mind. The Greek was willing to borrow, as Herodotus shows us, if it were only the practice of howling in religious ceremonies which he took from the Libyan.

The historian's free treatment of the history of Greek religion, the naturalness to him of his ancestors' borrowing rites and gods and the doctrine of immortality, illustrate the Greek mind and its ways for centuries. The old Egyptian, in Plato's *Timaeus*, says, "You Greeks are always children; you are always young in your souls", and it is true in more senses than he meant. They are always inquisitive, they are always asking questions, they are always interested, they are, as he says, always boys.[1] St Luke, in the *Acts*, gently

[1] It is not the boy of the English Public School, standardized into mental inertia, that is meant; but the natural boy, full of meddlesomeness, curiosity, and brightness. Strange that education should mean denaturing the best!

laughs at the Athenians as ever compelled to learn the
last new thing; and he echoes, in a way, the complaint
of the Corinthian in Thucydides, who, in a very
Athenian epigram, accuses the Athenians of never
being willing to let other people rest or to rest themselves. So it always was with the Greeks. From the
time when, after the centuries of darkness, their history
begins again in the Greek cities of the Asian shore, they
cannot be content in the parish in which they grow up.
They must wander—there are more reasons than one
for it—earth will not hold them, they chafe one another
in the little home town, they are curious of what is over
the hills and far away, and the sea calls them. So to
the sea they turn, and to exploration; and seamanship
is a constant exercise of the mind, a ceaseless practice
of individual judgment, an art that opens the door to
science, not least to astronomy. They plan colonies and
plant them; they expand all over the Mediterranean
and the Black Sea, city by city. It is not the migration
of the clan, as in the case of central Europe; it is not
the extension of an empire by force of arms; it is the
enterprise of city and citizen, and each colony becomes
a city, and, it may be, the centre of a new colonization.
Such men as Kolaios, who sailed to Gibraltar and beyond it to Gades; as that brother of Alcaeus, who
fought in Babylon; as the soldier of Colophon, or
Qolophon, as he spelled it himself, who went up the
Nile and carved his name on the legs of the Egyptian
king's colossi at Abu Simbel; are typical. They are
forever travelling, always interested in savage or barbarian, in any kind of man who does familiar things in
a new way, who betrays habits in government,
marriage, or diet, that challenge familiar usage.

21

Modern anthropologists have taught us a new respect for Herodotus, who is as much the father of their science as of history. "I travelled", says Herodotus, "for the sake of learning, for the sake of inquiry"; and he is interested in everything that meets his eye, soils, climates, customs, food, weather, burial habits, marriage habits, everything. Some readers have found him simple and childish, but that is careless reading. It is the simplicity of the essentially truthful mind, the bright interest of the boy always awake for the real.

Out of it all comes the Greek habit of mind, the passion for inquiry, and of course for discussion, the insistence on fact, and on the true cause. Herodotus carefully distinguishes between what he knows and what men tell him, and he apologizes more than once for making conjectures where proof is impossible, where the matter is unknown. Mr Marshall Macgregor says that "A harder, more precise thinker than Plato it will be difficult to discover". Polybius insists that nobody cares for what is contrary to nature or contrary to common conceptions of man; the human mind, he suggests, must have real facts and an intellectual apprehension of those facts.[1] Homer himself, according to Polybius, must base himself on fact; "To invent all carries no conviction and it is not Homer's way".[2] "How do you know that?" says Socrates to a young man;[3] "do you know it, or are you guessing?" "I am guessing", said the young man. "Very well", says Socrates, "when we are done with guessing and when we know, shall we talk about it then?" Aristotle

[1] Polybius xv, 36.   [2] Polybius xxxiv, 4, 4.
[3] Xenophon, *Memorabilia*, iii, 6, 11.

22

insists that writing too brilliant means obscurity, dark with excess of bright.[1] Socrates, Plato, Aristotle, they all insist on clear thinking, on definition, on knowing what you mean. We find the same thing in Marcus Aurelius two centuries after Christ, who thanks one of his teachers for training him to make a habit of reading precisely and refusing to be contented with a loose general impression.[2]

That, then, is the Greek habit of mind—interest, everlasting interest, ceaseless inquiry. "The un-examined life is not livable for a man", says Plato. But it is always into fact that the Greek will inquire, and everything must culminate in the actual truth, in the real explanation; some of us might call it an essentially modern temper. "Polymathy does not teach the mind", and "a hidden cause is better than an obvious one", says Heraclitus, lessons often for-gotten to-day. The Greek is always for sanity as opposed to caprice, and impatient of the monstrous fictions in which the Celt has at times delighted. When he sees the truth, like Phaedra, he will not let it go. Hence the surprising loyalty of the Greek to law in all that concerns art, a loyalty the stranger for his genius in making it consistent with freedom; other nations have had artists who stuck to rule at all costs, or broke all the rules in unchartered freedom. The Greek genius was to hold by both, by law and freedom. Nor this in art only; for in politics, for a while, the same two-fold loyalty prevailed, based on sense for fact. In art the Greek, let us say, is obedient to the laws of nature as he discovers them in the physical constitution of marble

[1] Aristotle, *Poetics*, 24, 23.   [2] M. Aurelius i, 7.

and in the principles of optics, but the soul of the artist must have freedom. When it comes to politics nature again has her laws, harder by far to discover, in the minds and hearts of men; the very existence of the state depends on recognizing these laws, and yet there must be a very real margin of freedom. Truth in marble, the ultimate fact in legislation, vision of the real, that is the Greek ideal. The Greek told a good many lies; at one time and another he had the lie upon his lips; but he would agree with Plato that the lie in the soul is the worst of lies.[1] It is doubtful if the Englishman would allow that; he insists on telling the truth, he has less passion for seeing the truth, he is described as "an adept in self-deception";[2] he loves a dim religious light, cultivates fog and calls it reverence. The standardization of opinion and education, as of social habits and clothing, the suppression of individual taste and thought, and at last of conscience, is the reproach of modern democracy. Ancient democracy was not sinless in this respect; freedom narrowed down from precedent to precedent, as Demos prevailed.

This application of reason to the facts of life, to the facts of the world, is never quite lost by the later Greeks. It is guaranteed to them by the beauty of their ancestors' creations, by art, poetry, philosophy— yes, and by another subtler thing, the happiness which beauty of itself gives to the human soul. "The soul", says Longinus, "takes wings at the sight of beauty, and soars up on high with glad uplift, as proud as if it had

[1] Plato, *Republic*, 382.
[2] A. E. Zimmern, in *Legacy of Greece*, p. 336.

itself produced what it sees." Beauty, we must remember, the idea of *charis*, of grace, was not reserved only for the statue or the temple; the Greek sought it and achieved it in the common things of life; in shape, colour, proportion and design he made his common vessels and implements beautiful, feeling, if he did not always talk about it, the essential relation between truth and beauty, discovered in common life.[1] The ideal citizen, Plato said, would be accustomed to play from childhood among things of beauty.[2] Study of the real led to deepening thought. Ploughman and seaman had to watch the stars, to know the great facts and laws of heaven. Thence rose Greek astronomy and Greek geography, and in both the individual did great things. Two facts we must remember about Greek astronomy; for twenty centuries Europe lived on a calendar of Greek making; and Copernicus himself was anticipated by Aristarchus of Samos. It was not a guess, but a reasoned verdict from observation that led this great man to conclude that the sun, not the earth, is the centre of the universe. Greek men of science, like medieval churchmen, rejected the idea, but it has prevailed; and this man reached the truth without a telescope, without any modern apparatus—a supreme victory of thought. Remember too the inquiry that haunts those earlier philosophers; what is the world-stuff—water or air or heat? The form of the question, the phrasing of the answer, is not our own,

[1] Cf. Pericles in Thucydides ii, 40, φιλοκαλοῦμεν μετ᾽ εὐτελείας. One may, perhaps, not too fancifully, compare the Hebrew idea, *Zech.* xiv, 21, "Every pot in Jerusalem and in Judah shall be holiness unto the Lord of hosts".

[2] Plato, *Republic*, viii, 558.

yet modern men of science are handling the same
type of question put in different words, but answered
at bottom in curiously similar conclusions.

It is the same instinct for the real whatever the
field; and who, like the Greeks, could discover the
beauty inherent in law and truth? Modern impatience,
weary of the triumphs of our fathers, may swing off into
a wild freedom; but humanity has a way of returning
to the Greek. Greek science stands opposed to magic.
Magic came into the Mediterranean world from
barbarians; it was an un-Hellenic thing; its professors
were Chaldaeans, Egyptians, Magians; the very name
of it betrays it as foreign. The Greek preferred to look
to the soil, to the water, to the climate, to the normal.
It is only in the decline of the Greek genius that
magic and astrology enter into the life of civilized man,
perhaps even then more in Roman than in Greek lands.

When it comes to the study of the human mind,
is it Nature, they ask, or is it training that makes us?
The question is still alive among ourselves. Pindar
is for Nature, as we saw; Plato stresses education,
uncomfortably recognizing that poets are not educated, but an inexplicable sort of divine madmen.
"Many are the wondrous things", says Sophocles,
"and none more wondrous than man." Why? Because
man has a mind in him that can grapple with everything in the world except death, and, above all, because
he understands law and frames states. "Man is the
measure of all things", says Protagoras—more ques-
tionably, as Plato shows. The Greek realizes the
grandeur and the greatness of man, and he will have
it that one of the greatest things in man is his unified

view of the world. Nature and philosophy are ever in agreement, as the Greek thinkers taught Juvenal.[1] Perhaps only in the sphere of religion does the Greek mind fail to develop, and we may hazard the reason. The Greek learned his religion from his womenkind, and left it to them in the main; and here he paid the penalty for locking his women up and keeping them untrained. It was Euripides who saw most clearly the wrong thus done to woman and felt its reactions.

But in politics it is another story. We see the Greeks grappling with the real in the sphere of government— the tribe, the canton, the city, the tyranny. Once again they recognized the significance of law, the necessity for government; but they would have it, as we saw, consistent with freedom, and the individual must not be crushed by the state as too often in Roman Empire and modern republic. All sorts of questions they ask; there is hardly any left for our age to add. What is the object of the state—economic or legal, justice or comfort, or something yet higher? What should rule in the state—tradition, interest, sentiment, passion or reason? Of course there are differences in the way problems affect us. The Greek wanted a share in government; the citizen of a big modern democracy knows he cannot have an effective share, and wishes to keep out. The danger to Greek freedom lay in tradition; to our freedom it lies in over-reform, over-regulation, excessive civil service; the Greek had practically no civil service. But then or now it is the same contrast between the individual and the state. To resume some actual Greek questions: What makes

[1] Juvenal xiv, 321, *nunquam aliud natura aliud sapientia dicit.*

the citizen? Is it ancestry, is it wealth, a stake in the country, is it residence, is it mere existence? The clash always possible between the claims of the family and the state did not escape the Greeks. Sophocles wrote his tragedy *Antigone* upon it. Plato, to safeguard the state, suggested the sinking of the family; but here Aristotle was the truer Greek, and refused to give up that great fact of nature. And all the questions come back to that central question, as poet and philosopher put it: what is man, what is the value of the individual?

They have a preference for the city-state. The vast size of Persia did not appear favourable to human freedom and dignity as the Greek understood it. In Egypt, as Herodotus sees, all is despotism, priestcraft, caste and tradition. There is nothing in either land that a Greek could recognize as citizenship, which is, after all, the highest function of man. As to the size of the ideal state, surely it must be a city, and not too big or mixed a city. Who, then, is to rule? Everybody, says Aristotle,[1] claims political ability. We also discover that. It is also worth noting, even if to some readers it seem slightly irrelevant, that Aristotle says exceptional people, who have more than our common share of wealth, birth, beauty and the like, find it hard to follow reason.[2] Surely those who are especially wealthy, or especially beautiful, should have a separate place in the state! The Greeks experiment with all varieties of constitution. They discard the clan for the state; and to reduce the power of the family, to eliminate the too-dominant individual, they try election of officials by lot; to secure the application of

[1] *Politics*, iv, 4, 18.   [2] *Politics*, iv, 11, 5.

sense to national problems and efficiency in business, they try tyranny; they try government by public meeting, and even the administration of justice by public meeting, in a blind faith in the average man; they try every kind of compromise except representative government, which of course to be effective requires paper and the press, neither of which was available; and last of all they try monarchy.

But they realize, as our contemporaries realize, that life does not consist entirely of political problems, that behind the political problems are the economic. As manufacture was still in the domestic stage, or, where the factory was beginning to come in, dependent on slave labour, modern industrial questions could hardly rise in the exact form in which we know them; but the Greeks raise and debate freely the question of the ownership of land. What is the proper thing to be done about land? Pisistratus established small landed proprietors all over Attica, at the cost, of course, of his political opponents, the big land-owners, the heads of the old families. Would it be a good thing periodically to break up the estates and to redistribute all landed property; and, if you did, should you include in the redistribution, or exclude from it, the slaves by whom the land has to be cultivated? The agricultural slave complicated the problem. When debt reaches a certain point in a city, is it desirable in the city's interests to cancel all debts, or perhaps some debts? Is all interest on money unnatural, as a naïve etymology of the word suggests? Is it natural "to take a breed for barren metal"? Should the rich expect to be taxed out of the common measure? Should the equipment of warships, for example, or the maintenance of the theatre, depend on special levies upon the property of the rich? Should all the poor be supported by taxation of the rich? It sounds horribly modern. In the later plays of Aristophanes we find the poet making fun of socialism of almost the nineteenth-century type, and of some developments of socialism which its twentieth-century opponents emphasize in their way. The greatest of all the sophists, of all the corrupters of youth, is, as Plato saw,[1] Demos himself. So he is still, but we disguise him as public opinion, common education, contemporary ideas.

All the problems we have noticed, and others, come up in the Greek world. They are all periodically raised, periodically discussed, sometimes with reason, sometimes with knives, as elsewhere. Greek democracy had not the advantage of bombs and revolvers, happily for mankind. The individual is always resurgent; once recognize him, as the Greek did, and how can you repress him? Teach him that it is his national duty to think, and think he will, for himself, and he will revolt against family, tyrant, democracy, or empire. The great ideal that most people have in politics, as Aristotle points out, is "to live every man as he likes".[2] Pure individualism could not go farther. Even in the most advanced societies it is difficult to be sure that in our hearts we have really got past that ideal yet. One political term of Greek life has a strange and a long history. The Assembly, the Ecclesia, was a word of appeal; and, curiously, at the very moment when it lost all meaning

[1] *Republic*, vi, 492 A.   [2] *Politics*, v, 9, 15.

in current political life, it was taken by the church and gained a new vitality. Even if we say that the church borrowed it, not from Athens, but from the Septuagint translation of the Hebrew scriptures, it is but one more stage in the story of what is still the most potent of words or of ideas. The Ecclesia of God is not exactly a Greek conception, but it witnesses to the fact that the Gospel had to reckon with the Greek.

Into this Greek world, full of interest and problem, full of question and debate, came the Persian; and his coming was a menace to Greek ideas of life, a challenge to democracy, and to the city-state. Could Greek democrats—amateurs in war, or little more, as the Persian prince Mardonius saw—could independent Greek cities, mutually jealous, withstand a united and all-conquering empire? Every sort of blunder was made, but the Persian "tripped over himself", and Themistocles and the Athenians saved Greece. Salamis was the decisive day. A line was crossed, such as modern generations have seen, on the 18th of June, 1815, or the 11th of November, 1918; a line crossed to a new era. It is a new Greece, with a new sense of power, dominating that glorious century, inspiring it; the divided nation had stood together for once and had driven back the greatest empire, and the most efficient, which the world had ever seen, and compelled it to recognize a point in the Mediterranean which it was not to pass. At the same time Greek genius, in the spheres of philosophy and beauty, reached its acme. The century is full of the sense of power in every phase of life. In the sphere of the world, where Greek genius had triumphed in using for its purpose land and sea

31

and sky, this sense of power degenerates into a crude and vulgar materialism. In the sphere of the city, proud of its victory over the Persian, proud of its federation of the Greeks, it changes into a harsh and narrow imperialism. In the sphere of philosophy, following upon the great thinkers Heraclitus and Pythagoras, we see sophistry in its worse sense. Against all this, there follows the great reaction of the Greek mind in Socrates, Euripides and Plato. Reaction to spiritual values is nowhere better to be seen than in the play of the *Trojan Women*, where the poet shows us in contrast Menelaus, the prince who has everything, and is nothing, and the fallen queen who has nothing and is Hecuba. To borrow a phrase from Longinus, which of the two would you rather be? It is a tremendous challenge that Euripides makes to wealth, success and cleverness; and the spiritual triumphs. It is a reaction from imperialism to humanity. Are you to cement victory, he asks in the play, by killing little children in cold blood? Plato puts the same sort of question in his own way in the *Gorgias*, and there and elsewhere he battles long (and that he must battle so often shows the pressure of the issue with the sophist) to bring Greece to a deeper mind, to a more fully thought-out life, to a more securely founded morality. He did not like democracy or "the democratic man"; they had killed Socrates; they represented the rule of chance human impulse against the eternal laws of God, of might against right. If Plato thinks much of the state, no man was so individualist as Socrates.

Such is the type of man that Greece breeds, a man

with a real conception of the state, not as an accident, not as an organization, but as something deeply and essentially rooted in human nature, the expression of God's conception of man, without which there cannot be man worth calling man. Nature should rule, the sophists said:

> Nature so willed, who takes no heed of laws.—[1]

There can be no state without laws, more sober thinkers urged; feeling their way to a deeper sense of law as the interpretation of Nature. Even before the Stoics the Greek keeps moving, as we saw, to the thought-out life, which means bringing state and law into some harmony with Nature, with essential human nature,[2] and with the Nature which is above all, behind all, and within all. In the centre stands the individual whom the Greek ever emphasizes, the man of power who thinks deeply upon government, morals, and beauty, who will miss nothing that is vital in them all; and, with all his passion for freedom, is loyal to what we must, borrowing a modern term, call law. Justice is one of the great words of Greece. The historian tells us of that conscientious Persian, King Cambyses, who found a judge judging unjustly, and had his skin taken off him, dressed, and made into a cushion cover for the judgment seat, and then appointed the dead judge's son to succeed him. It was an object lesson in justice, but rather too oriental for a more reflective people. Solon taught the Greek world to think in another way of justice, and the state, and all else. He

---

[1] Euripides, *Auge* fr. ἡ φύσις ἐβούλεθ᾽, ᾗ νόμων οὐδὲν μέλει. Contrast Herodotus vii, 104; Aristotle, *Politics*, iii, 11, 19.
[2] Cf. Aristotle, *Politics*, i, 3, 9; iii, 9, 12.

adjusted law to express the great progressive ideas of a people whom he trained to look without and to look within. The greatest economist of the ancient world, and a lover of men, he shaped the outlines of Athens. Athens might live on imported food, she might in commerce serve all the world and be served by it; and the state should be a brotherhood. Mr Zimmern has well said that Solon associated the idea of the state with kindness, and, as we saw, he emphasized the value of the individual as an asset. Out of his work comes that wonderful equation of the city and the citizen, the rule of law, the freedom of enterprise, and the love of beauty, which make Athens; and Athens, as her citizens said, was the education of Greece, and they were right.

Let us look at the resultant Greek man as we find him in the first century A.D., the Greek man, as he survives, who has to be won by Christ. If we to-day cannot write plays like Shakespeare, Shakespeare is still to be read, and we know that, if the right kind of play is to be written, it must be written in his way; the form may be modified, of course, but Shakespeare has taught all Englishmen for ever an attitude to life, a new sympathy for man and woman, a new humour; he has given us a sense of depth. Any new revelation of things human or divine has to stand the test of Shakespeare for us, even if there are no more Shakespeares. The Greek of the great days survived in much the same way for his descendants, an ideal nature, beyond them, but still their ideal. We have seen something of his experience; let us sum up our impressions of the type of man he has made.

He is, as Plato phrased it, "the spectator of all time and all existence".[1] More than that, adds Longinus, he takes part in the contest, in virtue of an unconquerable passion, implanted by Nature in the human soul, for the great thing, the diviner thing, so that not even the cosmos itself suffices for the soul, but it must pass beyond.[2] Curiosity, for the late Greek, and for some Christians, ranks almost as a vice; for the real Greek it is a virtue; for wonder, as Aristotle said, is the mother of philosophy, and the Greek loved both the mother and the daughter. As Celsus said in his attack on Christ, the barbarian has a certain gift for discovering dogma (he means religious truth); but the real value and meaning of the truth, on which the barbarian stumbles, it takes a Greek to understand. In a sense, Celsus is right; or we should have had no Christian theology. The Greek wonders, inquires, discovers, and then reflects. As Socrates said, he finds the unexamined life unlivable; he must relate everything to the real, to principle, to nature. *Physis*, Nature, is one of the greatest of Greek words; it is the Greek who gives us the conception that the ideal life of man is harmony with Nature. Man must live conformably, says the early Stoic, if he is to live aright, meaning conformably with himself; his life must be a unity; conformably with Nature, said the later Stoic, not in contradiction, but developing the thought, a nobler conformity, a higher unity. It is not impossible; all men, according to Aristotle,[3] more or less divine what is right or wrong; it is study of Nature that is to de-

---

[1] Plato, *Republic*, vi, 486 A.   [2] Longinus 35.
[3] Aristotle, *Rhetoric*, i, 13, p. 1373 b.

termine for them what they are feeling after. The state is real and essential because it is Nature's device for nurturing human life, which, without it, is impossible.

The great Greek social virtue is *sophrosyne*, a word always difficult to translate. It means anything and everything from sense to chastity. It means retention of a real hold on mind, and the application of it to everything moral, social and intellectual. The modern man lays a great deal of stress on the social virtues, some upon the moral virtues; but the Greek is ahead of us to this day in emphasizing the value of the intellectual virtues; and there lies a great problem. Would the Christian church go so far as Socrates in saying that unreflective virtue is as bad as vice? What is virtue? Let us think of it in two great Greek sentences. Protagoras said that man, or perhaps, more strictly, a man, any man, is the measure of all things; everything is relative to the individual. Well, yes, says Plato, in his *Laws*, so it has been said, but for us, at any rate, God is to be the measure of all things.[1]

So the Greeks of the great period looked at life, and thus looking at life, they made their great achievement, and it survived. The Greek habit of mind was developed into an educational system by Isocrates, a system under which all the world's thinkers were trained for centuries, and perhaps the best of them still are—at Oxford. The value of that outlook was to be read in the traditions of the Greeks, in their books, in their works of art. Everything must be examined; all the world is the proper study of man; there is no question which it is wrong for man to ask; Nature in

[1] *Laws*, iv, 716 c.

36

the long run must stand and deliver; God too must explain Himself, for did He not make man so? That is the Greek outlook, the inspiration of the great Greek type, one of the greatest types that the world has ever seen. With that type the early church confronted Christ. It was a question for two centuries whether Christ could win the Greek; and Christ did win him; and we may conclude our chapter with another sentence from Dean Inge: "The Reformation, on one side, is a return to Hellenism from Romanism".

III

ALEXANDER

Three centuries before the birth of Christ, Alexander's short life was over. Fourteen years was the span of his reign; and in it he altered the whole course of the world's history. To Europe and to a large part of Asia he brought new ways of looking at the world, a far wider range, a new sympathy for men of alien race, the need of a new philosophy, a new necessity for rethinking all the old conceptions of God.

In him men found a new type of personality, if not quite unexampled in history, yet never before seen in such brilliance and effectiveness. He gave mankind a new type of ruler with new ideals of government, and brought home to all men that they lived in a larger world than they had realized. One might almost say that he took his soldiers clean outside the map, and in doing so he created an immense series of new problems for the individual all over the world. Whether we look at the influence of his personality on his Successors, and on the Epigoni who succeeded them, on the Greek mind, on Greek imagination at large, and again on the Romans, on Caesar, for instance—"a lover of Alexander", as Strabo calls him[1]—on the Roman Emperors, and at last on the thinking of mankind, one is driven to ask the question whether he was not after all the world's greatest man.

[1] Strabo C. 59 a.

"As the pioneer of Hellenic cultivation", wrote Edward Freeman,[1] "he became in the end the pioneer of Christianity"; and, on the next page, "the victories of Christian Emperors, the teaching of Christian Fathers, the abiding life of the tongue and arts of Greece far beyond the limits of old Hellas, perhaps the endurance of Greek nationality down to our own times, all sprang from the triumphs of Alexander". And to relate our subject to our particular thesis we may turn once more to Wilamowitz: "Gewiss vollstreckt er (St Paul) unbewusst das Testament Alexanders indem er das Evangelium zu den Hellenen bringt". Assuredly, he says, St Paul is executing, though unconsciously, the testament of Alexander in bringing the Gospel to the Hellenes.

What sort of man was this, then? His face is familiar on gems and coins and in sculpture; and the archaeologists tell us that the close study by sculptors of the peculiar character of Alexander's face—his heavy brow and deep-set eye and the fiery glance of genius akin to madness—told upon all their other work. Alexander's features shaped the portraits of princes and the ideas of artists.[2]

Not less striking, or less formative for mankind, was the man's character. When Mr Delisle Burns suggests that Alexander had a primitive mind, it does not sound perhaps like praise. Grote puts it in another way, telling us that his character recalls those of the heroes of legendary Greece. When we turn to our ancient writers, Strabo tells us that he was a lover of

[1] Freeman, *Essays*, vol. ii, pp. 204–5.
[2] Ernest Gardner, *Handbook of Greek Sculpture*, pp. 436, 437.

Homer; Plutarch speaks of his love of reading in general; and one and another tell us of the marvellous box, the richly carved coffer, that he found in the camp of the Persian king, and reserved for the carriage of his *Iliad* across Asia.[1] He read Homer from the Hellespont to the Panjab, and thence to Babylon.

The pedigree, that for generations before his birth the Greeks had preserved, proclaimed that he was descended from Achilles and from Andromache; the blood of the great heroes of Homer ran in his veins; and he believed it with conviction, with the passion of the Highlander for the clan of whom he comes. Through other lines he was descended from Perseus and from Herakles, and he was conscious of it. Call it what you will—there are those, perhaps Saxons, who may style it Romanticism; the Celt will have a tenderer name for it—but to be conscious of such a descent from such men and such women is no light thing in the shaping of character. He is the child of Achilles, and he loves to think of it; he loves to mould himself upon his ancestor; he loves to read of him. Sometimes his imitations of him are a shade external, but at the same time there is in him a great deal of the quality of his ancestor. Think of his chivalry to the fallen foe, to Darius, to Porus. "How am I to treat you?" he says to Porus. "Like a king", says Porus; and Alexander is won by the answer and treats him like a king. It was in that spirit that Achilles received Priam.

He is a mystic. What the god Ammon said to him no one knows; but it influenced his mind and shaped his actions. We can see a reminder of it in the ram's

[1] Plutarch, *Alex.* 8; 26; Macchiavelli, *Prince*, ch. 14.

horn, like a larger curl among his hair on the coins. He is conscious that he is the instrument of the gods. There is something in him like the Calvinist of the great period. Carlyle at least said that it was Calvinism that made all the heroes; and Alexander (descended from Achilles) is the chosen vessel of heaven. *Ego poscor Olympo*, as Virgil's Aeneas says. To understand him, we have to realize these lines of communion with the great, these two avenues to greatness; for both of them mark him out from ordinary men.

But to turn to the more common thoughts and movements of man's mind, the historians remark his great powers of self-restraint and self-government. That he drank to excess on occasion every one knows, but it was on occasion only; he was no wine-bibber. All antiquity remembered his iron self-repression where women were concerned. Some writers have tried to magnify his generals, and attribute much of the credit of his movements and victories to them; but he was the driving force behind them, he over-ruled them. A night attack was a plan that might do for Parmenio; for Alexander it would not do; "he would not steal his victory".[1] He refused Parmenio's proposal of a night attack; he would have a set battle, an affair of bloodshed and loss of life, the destruction of thousands. Yes, but it told Darius and all Asia, and all the world, the Greeks included, that they need fight no more; a successful night attack would have had no such message; and the soldier of genius saw what the merely effective man missed. He was practical, in-

[1] The battle of Gaugamela; cf. Arrian iii, 10; Plutarch, *Alex.* 31; D. G. Hogarth, *Philip and Alexander*, p. 203.

tensely practical. He did his own thinking as a soldier, but he had the gift for organization, a different thing from vision—as Europe learnt at Paris in 1919; and to all he added a unique capacity for action. A master of strategy, a master of tactics, he was, moreover, a born leader of men; he knew how to win, to hold and to lead them. He was not for nothing a lover of symbolism; the greatest of modern soldiers has commented on Alexander's skill in the appeal to the imagination. It is imagination again and again that makes the great leader, that makes the *morale* of his followers. Napoleon was right. A ceaseless organizer, a tireless worker, a master of detail, he instinctively knew human nature, and how to move it. Plutarch speaks of the endless letters he wrote to his friends telling of the work that was heaped upon himself.

But he was far more than even a soldier of the utmost genius. The whole management of the empire, which was growing larger and larger every year, its government, its administration, its finances, its commerce, the foundation of new cities, the fusion of peoples, the co-ordination of everything, were part of his task. Everything was the King's work. Little wonder that he wore himself out, and succumbed to a fever after fourteen years of kingship. It all helps us to measure the greatness of the King.

He was a man, but he soon became the subject of legend. The cheerful story is told by Plutarch[1] how an historian of the day made his history of Alexander more picturesque by an amazing and miraculous episode, and how he read his manuscript to one of the

[1] Plutarch, *Alex.* 46.

hero's generals and successors; "and", said King Lysimachus to the historian, "where was I, when all this was happening?" The miraculous came into the story in the lifetime of his friends; it came in more and more afterwards. His story became a legend, a romance; we are told that there are eighty versions of the Alexander romance in twenty-four languages, from Ethiopic westwards. The great campaign is halted to bring the conqueror into Jewish history, remodelled to admit him; he is taken to Jerusalem. The story of Alexander was one of the four great cycles of hero stories of the Middle Ages. Troy, Charlemagne and Arthur are the other three. I cannot but think that all this affected "books of chivalries", in which case Don Quixote himself may be a lineal descendant of Alexander the Great: he too modelled himself on a hero and a book; and the same nobility is to be seen in the one and the other. Historians are sometimes too contemptuous of legend and myth and romance. How, we may ask them, does a man get into legend, or become a legend, and through legend touch the imaginations and hearts of mankind? It always, or almost always, means some strong distinctive human quality, or, if not, at least some astounding adventure; in Alexander's case there are both, and it is his character that makes his adventure.

To turn back from legend to fact, Alexander is one of the supreme fertilizing forces of history. He lifts the world into new habits of mind and brings in a new epoch. He gives science and civilization a new scope. Freeman speaks of him as the "ardent searcher after knowledge, eager to enlarge the bounds of human science and to search out distant lands"; and we remember how he himself explored both the channels of the Indus, fighting his way down and back again, until he sailed on the Indian Ocean; "I think", says Arrian, "he did it to be able to say he had sailed on the Indian Ocean". Who would not "stare at the Pacific"? He sent back from the East specimens of strange new creatures to Aristotle. Incidentally, he gave Greece a new speech, for the *koine* is the outcome of his blending all Greek breeds and dialects in a new distribution over a wider world. He brings in also the craving for a new spiritual unity. The ideal city-state was still of interest to his teacher—a curious illustration of the detachment of the academic mind; for, while Aristotle speculated, Alexander was in fact so acting as to change the face of the world and to make the city-state a mere anachronism; and the King was providing that stimulus from the actual world which prompted the Stoic to conceive of another ideal state altogether, the cosmos, the city of Zeus, the greatest conceivable unity of all. Two of the chief of Alexander's thoughts survive to this day—the divine kingship seen in Caesar and Pope; and that universalism in thought, philosophy and religion, which we meet first in Stoicism and then in our own religion. Whatever were his own thoughts as to his nature, his kinship with the god, or his own divinity, he did not claim divine honours; but it is memorable that he was the first Greek king to whom they were given. "To me", says Arrian[1] long after, "it seems impossible that such a man was born without the divine, a man like no other among men."

[1] vii, 30, 2.

44

Alexander's great conception seems to have been the combination of all the world's best, not a mere dreamer's Utopia, not a heavenly "Republic", like Plato's, small, remote, despotic and closed against ideas, but the actual world that he traversed and explored, united into one state whose citizens were the men whom he knew, men of every tribe and habit and outlook. We have to remember always that he did live among them, and that, like Herodotus and one or two other exceptional Greeks, he was one of those gifted men who recognized the new type of greatness when he saw it; a man, who, when he met the foreigner, took in his significance and realized the new values to humanity in the type he had not met before. Was it possible to make one world of it, to do away with the enmity, the walls of partition, the barriers that have divided state from state, race from race, to induce Greek and Persian, instead of fighting one another, to share their great gifts, and, uniting all, to blend every type of greatness in an ideal man, in a united world? What a conception!

The two great things in this are the old Greek ideas re-interpreted on a new plane and with a new imagination—the unity of the world and the value of the individual man. That is our problem to this day. He thinks in terms of the whole world far more than any Greek before him. He is emancipated from much that circumscribed all Greeks in their conception of the idea of the *polis*. His cardinal ideas are expansion and comprehension—geographical, commercial and political expansion, comprehension in politics, in the affairs of the market, in culture and all that makes the higher life. By his understanding of men and his power of uniting men, by his travels, his conquests, his explorations, his dreams, he succeeded in bringing home to men the unity of the intellectual world; and more than any other man he broke down the barriers that kept men and races apart. It became impossible to think of the world and of human life but as he thought of it. I do not know whose is the phrase which was quoted by Mahaffy, but "the marriage of Europe and Asia" is his design. The historians tell us how he tried to bring it about by marrying ten thousand of his Macedonians to ten thousand girls of Persian, Indian and other oriental origin, reinforcing their charms and his theories with good concrete dowries. One is always a little sorry for a human being who is made a symbol for genius to use, and one wonders what became of these ten thousand poor symbols when the great dreamer died at Babylon. The Greek political system is replaced by a larger; but, in spite of the grumbles and the fears of his Macedonians, he does not merely superimpose the old Persian system upon Greek citizens and his own clansmen; he never called himself King of Kings; he was not the heir of Darius; his kingdom is different. It is a new world, and there is to be a new government for the new empire; and all this time he never lost faith in the supremacy of Hellenic culture,[1] in the Greek conviction of the value of the development of the individual. The new empire was to be founded on that very ideal. Was it possible? Possible or not, when St Paul wrote to the Ephesians he used language to describe a new order

[1] W. S. Ferguson, *Greek Imperialism*, 135.

for the human race which this king might have taken in large measure to picture his own ideals. Was it mere accident this, a chance coincidence, or is there a real relation between the two idealists?

There is one thing which the practical and the matter-of-fact love to point out, and they are always right; the ideals of genius always break down. The empire of Alexander vanished. Yes, but the ideas of Alexander remain. But are they compatible, are they possible? Life seems to call for organization, and then dies of it. Where you have a huge political fabric, what becomes of culture? Can a great monarchy impose it on its subjects, can a vast democracy be sure of "educating its masters"? Is culture to be organized, the soul to be standardized? After all the hopes formed for the United States of America, what becomes of the individual there? Is he not apt to be lost in the organization, standardized, sterilized, atrophied? Is it not sadly true that only once, in Athens, Demos really believed in culture, and then not for long? Is it not true that a civil service is in essence the negation of that freedom on which the Greek insisted, the very breath of life for culture?

A few words, however, on the system of Alexander. There was to be one government for the world, but that government was to be sustained by new cities, by the extension of commerce, by the spread of Greek civilization. He was to use to the full the moral energy of the Greek character, to make it available all over the world for the preservation of his empire; and in a manner he succeeded there. The monarchic power once held by the Persian king was to remain, but he planned to have free institutions in municipal government. The city was the *nidus* of Greek culture, and he planted Greek cities from the Nile to the Indus. His idea, his influence, survived; his conception of humanity did not die. Nor did his ideal of culture die; it lived and altered the habits of races, not indeed for ever, but an ideal that lives among mankind for five hundred years is a great contribution to mankind; and the Renaissance brought back Alexander's ideal of Greek culture to new life. Something of his love of man survived to temper the despotic sway of his Successors who, with all their faults, never quite relapsed to the standards of Persian monarchy; they held to his ideal of royal magnanimity; they believed in his Greek cities, and founded their own Antiochs and Apameias; and Rhodes in her misfortunes could be thankful for royal generosity on the scale of Alexander. Thus the ideas of Alexander assert themselves again.

In a later chapter we must return to his cities. He is said to have founded seventy, not all, like those of the Greeks, on the sea. Kandahar is very far from the sea. He not only founded new cities, but he refounded, enlarged and hellenized old ones, cities where Greeks, Macedonians and natives should live together and modify one another. It is not the subordination of everything to the Greek; that was not his ideal, and it could not be. In fact, we observe this tempering of the Greek in his turn by the rest; the wife of the lower race had, as she ever has, too great an influence. Alexander admired the Iranian noble; the great landowning noble, familiar in Persia, and known to us through Herodotus and Xenophon, was one of the great types. Hellas, with all her gifts, did not greatly succeed in breeding gentlemen. Perhaps to breed them, land and generations and monarchy are needed. Alexander was quick to recognize the dignity and worth of this type; and he wished to keep it; but it is very doubtful if it survived his immediate Successors. His cities were not quite like the cities of the Greeks; probably there was no council or assembly in most of them, and they were all amenable to a law which they did not make, that came down in royal rescripts, unwelcome often, as that was which commanded the cities of old Greece to recall their exiles. But justice was administered by law-courts, more or less Greek, and more or less responsible to the King, better and steadier courts than any assembly of old Demos, but administering much the same law, reconceived and remodelled with a wider outlook. Along with it there are the great features of the Greek city that gave the stamp to all these foundations, his own and those of his successors; the theatre, with the great plays from the past that still survive, music, literature, sculpture, architecture, and the Greek cult of the body in athletics; all of them Greek ideas, and all given to the world by this man of genius.

If the plan of intermarriage failed, or only succeeded to destroy Greek influence, we have abundant evidence of the new influence of mind on mind in Alexander's empire. There are few things more interesting, I think, in the study of art than to traverse a certain gallery in the Calcutta Museum, and to see the Buddha story touched by the Greek spirit on one side of the room, and Hindu conceptions of art and godhead on the other. Buddha in the Swat Valley came to look like a Greek god. In Greece one of the foremost of influences after Alexander was a long, lean, dusky-skinned Semite from Tyre, called Zeno. The Apocrypha is full of Greek books written by Jews. No Jew ever spoke in Hebrew of God as "the first author of beauty", or called the cosmos "the champion of the righteous".[1] These are thoroughly Greek expressions, Greek ways of looking at God and the world; the old religion has gained something by its contact with the Greek mind, and lost something, too.

After his fourteen years of activity, Alexander died of fever at Babylon, in 323 B.C. The Greek orator, Demades, said that Macedon after his death was like the blinded Cyclops in his cave. What was to happen to the world? What was Macedon to do? The prayer that every man of genius should pray is, "Save me from my disciples", but the only way to carry on Alexander's government—his heir was not yet born—was that it should be in the hands of his generals. That half-oriental heir lived to be ten or twelve years old and was murdered; the royal family was blotted out; and the generals became kings in one part of the world or another; three at least of them founded dynasties. Democracy was outworn; city-states held out no hope of unity; the world was full of armies; it could only be governed by kings.

On the whole, considering that it was human society and centralized administration, the government is generally thought to have been good—at any rate better than what went before it, as we shall see. Here

---

[1] *Wisdom of Solomon*, 13, 3; 16, 17.

and there cities were linked up in Leagues, which contributed ideas to the federal governments of the present day, something to America, something to Canada, something to the British Empire. But more significant for the period than the Leagues were the hereditary monarchs. Leagues or monarchs, they depended, like the Greek cities, and the Persian kings before them, on mercenary armies. Mercenary soldiers have a bad name, and the ancient evidence suggests it is not undeserved. But, to be just to them, under the Hellenistic kings these mercenary armies made war something of a science. The types of troops had multiplied with very specialized training, and Alexander had shown once for all that in scientific warfare, with its varied types, victory was won by brain rather than by brute force; the old days of competitive massacre were over; it meant a mitigation of war. These soldiers were no patriots, with the hate that nerves patriotism; they fought for paymasters, not to kill one another, but to put one another in the position of not being able to fight; the spear was held up and the battle was over; and captors and captives would meet as old friends of last year. It is worth remembering that the big armies meant larger empires, and very generally in the world's history larger empires have meant larger areas of peace. The world was governed a good deal by garrisons, Greece by its "three fetters", as the Macedonian called the great fortresses. It is an age of royal rescripts and manifestos. "All kings", says Polybius[1], "begin with fine talk about Greek freedom." They all did, and some-

[1] xv, 24, 18.

times it meant very little; Polybius later on[1] gives us the curious picture of two rival liberators of Greece. Great kings and great kingdoms and the balance of power[2] implied ambassadors and diplomacy, which became more of an art than ever. In the next chapter we shall meet one of the astutest of these ambassadors, and we have not to forget that the use of ambassadors always implies some thought of peace.

But the greatest factor in securing the peace of the world was the general recognition that everything was changed from of old, and that there was no going back. Whatever may be said about the Successors, and their personal characters, and their wars of ambition, carried on at the cost of the tax-payer—but waged in fact by the mercenary soldier, for whom tears are not often shed—the Successors kept before mankind the idea of the unity of the world. Every one of them was "king" not of this or that part of the world, but simply "king", and this plain term carried the suggestion that, when he came to his own, he would be king of the whole heritage of Alexander. Mankind accepted the situation; even in Alexander's days Aristotle wrote[3] that the habit now was not even to care about equality—all men sought dominion, or, if conquered, were willing to submit to it. The change of mood contributed to world peace. In the medieval world something of this idea of unity survived from the old Roman Empire which we have quite lost; we live in an age ever more conscious of nationality, which after Alexander is less and less a factor for centuries.

[1] xx, 8, 1. [2] An amusing chapter in Polybius (xxix, 7).
[3] *Politics*, iv, 11, 19.

In its way this conception of unity was something of a protection to the world. Even apart from ideas the kings were very real protectors. They protected civilization against the barbarians of the north and of the east, especially against our kinsmen, those "late born Titans" the Gauls. Like the later Goths, if more barbarous, the Gauls descended upon the world, and scared it, not least by their habit of fighting stark-naked and yelling all the time—the tallest and most beautiful of men in the world, as Polybius says, and as we can believe who recognize the breed in the famous statue of the Dying Gaul, which commemorates one great victory over them. The kings also put a stop in large measure to the wars between Greek cities, which now meant nothing, and they were the real protectors of mankind against the socialism of the day and the decline of human ideals that it would have involved. At the same time it is lamentably true that their wars among themselves were calamitous.

But we have to look at the Successors and their descendants, because as men, consciously modelling themselves on an ideal, they are a new type which affected the world. At the end of *Antony and Cleopatra* the Roman soldier breaks into the chamber and finds Cleopatra dead and turns to the waiting-woman; "Charmian, is this well done?" It is a sign of the new age that the waiting-woman of the queen has such an utterance as Shakespeare gives; he took it, with much else, from Plutarch:

> It is well done, and worthy of a princess
> Descended of so many royal Kings.

Alexander gave the world the prince type. Bagehot,

in his book *The English Constitution*, tells us that there are certain very obvious advantages in monarchy; it is an eminently intelligible form of government, and it is spectacular. The princes were intelligible to the world; they were certainly spectacular; they were magnificent creatures, magnificent in their outlooks, their pageants and their wastefulness. Look at the pageants of Alexandria and Antioch, described by Polybius and others. Look at the libraries the kings founded, at the enormous endowments they gave to culture and to science, at their royal bounties to cities in distress. There is a new conception of the duties of a prince. One of them is to hold and to defend his kingdom. There is great variety among the princes, and they are constantly interesting. Take for example Ptolemy the Thunderbolt, whom most people were glad to avoid and whom one cannot admire; Demetrius the Besieger; Pyrrhus, the most chivalrous perhaps of them all, who gave the Romans the conception of chivalry and grandeur which he had learnt from Alexander and which the poet Ennius made eternal in Latin poetry. Then again there are the great saviours of ancient learning and literature, the luxurious Ptolemy II, and Attalus, in his rather commercial kingdom of Pergamum. Antigonus Gonatas was a philosopher king; and few of them could rival Antiochus Epiphanes in interest; who did so much as he for Judaism? Among them there were really great rulers. What is more, the women of these great houses were often as brilliant and as unscrupulous as the men. Cleopatra herself is only one, if the greatest, of a wonderful series of princesses.

But, alas! it is true, as Cavour said, that the worst chamber is better than the best ante-chamber. There is too much of the royal chamberlain. It was a doubtful gain when, in that ancient world, aristocracy was succeeded by bureaucracy, by a breed of efficient people, whom the Roman Empire once more developed, to the destruction of initiative, liberty, spirit, and at last of the Empire itself. There are great drawbacks in monarchy, as the ancient world found. Mr Gladstone once said that "the greatest difficulty of constitutional monarchy is the education of the heir apparent"; and when his father keeps a harem, and it is not quite certain who the heir will be, the difficulties are greater. War, also, as we have seen, was far too frequent; and there were amazing accidents in war and peace, in battlefield, in fortress and in harem, all of them giving a stronger emphasis to the new goddess, Fortune.

But we must look briefly at the people themselves. The Hellenistic world of course was not stationary; there is change and movement, advance and decline from Alexander to Augustus, but certain common factors are to be recognized. The fall of Persia, and the liberation of the royal hoards, meant immense new wealth, and the reactions of that wealth, in the Greek world, with change in standards of living, in the predominance of races and districts, with new economics and new methods in industry. Alexander opened new routes for trade; there is new imagination in commerce, "the golden journey to Samarkand", the voyage to India. All these things count. There are royal law courts at last, as we saw; and western Asia revives when freed from the Persians. There follows, from Alexander's colonization, his diffusion of the Greeks, a new freedom to move about all the world; Greece is abandoned, as New England is abandoned, for fresh woods and pastures new. We have also to remember—what many readers of ancient history constantly forget—the steady increase of the population all round the Mediterranean. There is a great rise in numbers in all the races, and civilization is spreading westward into Italy, and from Italy into Spain, and northward too, though we hear less of that. But a gold currency in pre-Roman Britain, modelled on that of the Hellenistic kings, is evidence of movement.

It is often suggested that the Hellenistic age is one of decline. There is an interesting discussion in Longinus as to the effect of the loss of freedom upon literature, with an alternative view that luxury may be as fatal. He wrote in the Roman Empire, but we should keep his question in mind when we study the earlier Hellenistic period. Mr E. N. Gardiner puts it that this was not an age of ideals but of experiments in religion, in politics, in art and in science. In the Hellenistic world there seems to have been more refinement, more feeling, among a larger section of society; and there was more education, but it was standardized and it suggests Dr Johnson's remark about Greek in Scotland, where everybody had a little and nobody a bellyful. If standardization in culture is not perhaps its negation, it is surely so in literature. Mahaffy defended Hellenistic literature, but Benjamin Jowett spoke of it as "this monotony of literature without merit, without genius and without character". Apart from Theocritus, the taste of the world, ancient and

modern, confirms this severe judgment. Dr Ernest
Gardner says that "an age of decadence is often an age
of study and criticism, and the Hellenistic period is
perhaps the most conspicuous example". Everyone,
I think, would feel that in vivid fresh interest it is far
below the Greece of Thucydides and of Euripides. But,
all the same, it is still a living Greece busy with other
things. There is an advance of humanity, if there is a
decline of taste. If there are constant acts of cruelty,
man is beginning to love the child, the slave, the
flower, more than was common before; and that is not
altogether decline. There are no politics in the literature, there is no polity in the world, there is no parish
which can set the name of Acharnae in poetry for
all time. Every man lives in the world; but the world,
while a good place in itself, is not like Grantchester in
the poem we remember; it is good enough, but too big
to love. Genius is declining, but learning is advancing,
and we remember Pindar's comment. If there is no
Homer to write a new *Iliad*, there is an Aristarchus to
edit the old *Iliad*; and science makes great strides
forward. Perhaps literature and science rarely advance together; each needs its own background, and
the same background does not suit both.

In art there are new modes. There are more people
interested in art, people wanting art in their houses,
statues, statuettes, paintings on their walls; and the
subjects they like are taken from this mythology. They
like pictures in relief and pictures of country life; they
love models of children; and these are well done. The
little boy with the goose is a little boy, while, in the old
days, the infant god in the arms of the Hermes of

Praxiteles is not a baby. Again, they like the portrait, they like the colossus. They gave us the Dying Gaul, the Aphrodite of Melos. The dominant art of the period is architecture, and architecture with new ideas; in old days the thing of beauty might be set down by itself regardless of its surroundings, but now art studies the general effect as opposed to the individual thing. When one thinks of the wide diffusion of this interest in art, and of the quickening that even industrial reproduction of art may mean—that even a halfpenny newspaper may mean—there is something to be said for Wendland's view, who maintains that "in a certain sense Greek history reaches its highest point in this period, when Hellenism reaches the consciousness of its great task in the spiritual conquest and education of the peoples". It is not, I think, to be abruptly dismissed as an age of decline.

What has become of the citizen? In Athens we remark the equation of *polis* and *polites*. In this age the citizen is becoming a subject. There is a great new type, bestriding the world like a colossus. There are great things to do, wonderful things to do, but not enough men to do them, not enough people educated for it, not enough inspired. The individual is a little frightened of the world in which he lives; he is so startled by the ups and downs of princes and leagues, the disappearance of kings and dynasties. Is it τύχη, is it Fortune? or is it Fate? Is it pure fluke, or is it unbreakable order, which makes and breaks the rulers of the world? These are the two great lines of thought that prevail; and it is significant of much, that neither word is found in the New Testament.

58

The change in city life, the transformation of citizen into subject, leaves the individual isolated; and his contemporaries did not greatly inspire him. He could read the geography of Eratosthenes, of course; but to read that, or a commentary on Homer, is not quite what Achilles would want to do. It is possible for political conditions to produce intellectual atrophy; and our great democracies may discover, as those great princedoms discovered, that a citizen can only thrive imperfectly if cut in two. Can you think, if you are only half a man, a decimal of a man? In most great modern nations, we all tend, as in the Hellenistic kingdoms, to develop "all on one side" as Touchstone said, "like an ill-roasted egg". And he had a brief description of that condition, which was probably correct. Men lose confidence in themselves and in the world. Polybius emphasizes the decline of the birthrate in Greece. What was the cause of it? Why did the population fall? Was it that the Greeks migrated to the new cities, as New England has migrated westward? Was it luxury, as in our day we see that a motor car is worth many children? Or was it sheer despair? New fears and new facts challenge the Reason anew. That huge world, the cosmos, was too much; there was nothing between the individual and the cosmos, no shelter in place or city or nation. New questions rise as to god and man, the soul and immortality. There are new ideas, new conceptions of morality; there is some disappointment as to man's government of the world, some disappointment as to God's government of the world. The Stoic and the Epicurean have to teach man how to live anew, with a minimum of relation to God.

But above all new religions arose. Athena on the Acropolis is a long way off when you are bivouacked on the Bias; the scope of Athena, like that of most Greek gods, had been too local. The Hebrew David complained to King Saul of those who would drive him out of the heritage of Jehovah into the territory of other gods; and the same question confronted the Greek at the world's end. As he thinks of one world, one empire, one government, the little local gods look queer and old and very parochial; and he begins to think of one god, or one goddess, who can make one universe of it as Alexander ruled one world —one divine something, whether Fate, or cosmos, or what? God or the divine or whatever it is must have the range of Alexander; what of his ideals? There is a new willingness to inquire as to the gods of the various races, and if George Finlay was right (and he probably was) in saying that the Greeks used their new advantages for acquiring religious knowledge very sparingly, at any rate Berossus and Manetho gave them something, right or wrong, about the religions of Babylon and of Egypt, and we can see the effect in the reflexions of Plutarch and his school. The Septuagint is a monument still in our hands of the translation of a religion into a new language, the outcome of a changing religious experience, the promise of a new day.

There then is the new world, with its fears and questions, the world in which the New Testament came into being. Two questions are left. Is Reason as sovereign, at any rate in the latter end of this period, as she was in the great age of Greece? And is the individual, cramped and atrophied, bullied by civil servants, professors and priests, scared by Fate and Fortune, equal to grappling with Reason? These are the vital questions, and in each case the answer involves some sadness.

IV

THE ROMAN

In the Middle Ages the University of Cambridge was
a poor, lowly and obscure affair compared with
Oxford. In the sixteenth century a great change came.
Their rôles were entirely reversed, and Cambridge
supplied England with her great men, with her statesmen, her poets, her reformers and her martyrs; and
there are those who suggest that the change was due
in some large measure to the fact that, when the
Renaissance came—the real rebirth of Europe, Oxford
chose to stand on the ancient paths and Cambridge
identified herself with the study of Greek, led by
Erasmus, and with the newer movements of life and
thought. And from that day, perhaps, it is not too
much to say that Greek has been more loved at
Cambridge than Latin, the Greek than the Roman;
for even Virgil as a rule finds no exponent, but Greek
plays are acted and Greek philosophy and Greek
history shape the thoughts.

Then a Greek shall put the question for us; and it is
nowhere more strongly put than in the famous pro-
logue of Polybius. Writing somewhere about the year
150 B.C., he calls the attention of the Greek world, in
a very striking passage, to the change that fifty-three
years brought over the whole Mediterranean world.
In fifty-three years the whole face and future of the
world have been so altered that one power is every-

where dominant. Rome had not, indeed, annexed all the kingdoms, but her control was world-wide. A man must be dull indeed, Polybius suggests, he must even be lacking in moral quality, who does not wish to understand this amazing transformation and the predominance of Rome, all achieved in the space of fifty-three years. What is there to explain it? That is the thesis of his work. It is not events, says Polybius, that are interesting, but their causes; and he finds moral causes for Rome's supremacy. Hence his suggestion that to be incurious argues moral failure.

Down to the days of Hannibal, Greece had been markedly inattentive to Rome; the Greeks looked eastward, very naturally, as a result of their history; civilization had lain that way; Persia lay there; and Alexander had re-emphasized the East anew. So, Polybius says, a Greek author would write you a universal history, and gaily knock off Rome and Carthage in a couple of pages each. And then in the Hannibalic War, a Greek statesman, strangely enough an Aetolian, called the attention of his people in so many words to "the clouds gathering in the west". He was right; the clouds were indeed gathering in the west, and before long the storm moved over the Adriatic and broke. Three familiar anecdotes, quite probably true, at all events with much truth in them, will illuminate the new discoveries.

First, there is the famous story of the report of Kineas to Pyrrhus, when he came back from Rome and told him that he had seen an "assembly of kings" —it was the Roman Senate. To many it may seem a mere anecdote, a piece of Roman bragging. Yet when one realizes who Kineas was, what had been his life's work, the age he lived in, the people whom he knew, and what he found in Rome, the story does not seem at all absurd or unlikely; it is true. It is true, whether Kineas said it or not. Kineas went to Rome to see a senate—he had seen many senates in Greece. An old diplomat, an agent of kings, practised in the handling of men (for the very significant praise of Pyrrhus is recorded), he knew the sort of thing he was going to meet; and he did not meet it. Instead of the Greek βουλή, *bule*, with its mass of chattering and excitable nonentities, perhaps elected by lot to secure that there should be the minimum of decisive brains present at any meeting (there were, of course, other types in Greece), he met a really deliberative body made of ex-magistrates, men who had been elected to responsible positions by their fellow-citizens, entrusted with the greatest thing that Rome knew, the *Imperium*, who had handled the business of a great state; many of them had been elected again and again to higher magistracies; many, moreover, had grown up in families of like tradition. They were men indeed, very far from being the nobodies of a Greek council. When Kineas spoke of them as an assembly of kings, he was speaking the language that he and Pyrrhus understood, for they had lived in a world of kings—the eastern Mediterranean; they had personally known the great Successors of Alexander; they had associated with great men, who carried national responsibility, who handled kingdoms and huge armies, who thought in the large and were realists. It was the moment in the world's history when the word *king* carried most

content. To these men Kineas compared the Roman
senators; and when he told his master that the Roman
Senate was an assembly of kings, he was right. The
Roman senator was one of the best types that the
world knew, or had ever seen, or perhaps was ever to
see again.

A few years later Pyrrhus left Sicily, and, according
to a famous story, which Plutarch preserves, he said to
his officers as they left: "What a wrestling ground, my
friends, we are leaving for the Romans and the
Carthaginians!" He saw that the age-long quarrel
between Greek and Carthaginian was to be settled
by a new power, that Sicily was lost for ever to Greek
sovereignty; and he seems to have divined, as Milo,
his captain at Tarentum, some years later divined,
that the future would be with the Roman, and better
so. In any case, no Greek, who knew the story of
Sicily, would wish to aggrandize the Carthaginian.
Ptolemy II of Egypt made diplomatic overtures, we
are told, to Rome, when he heard of the failure of
Pyrrhus. He too recognized that there was a new
power in the west, a Mediterranean power, to be
reckoned with, by the Carthaginian, and, no doubt,
in time, by the Macedonian.

A full century or more later, Antiochus Epiphanes
marched upon Egypt with an army—there was no
great moral issue involved, it was a mere war of
ambition—and there landed somewhere near his camp
a Roman senator with a small group of secretaries and
attendants. He made his way to the king, and they
met somewhat informally and exchanged greetings.
Antiochus had lived thirteen years as a hostage in

Rome, and they talked of this and that; and why had he come? Popillius Laenas replied that the Roman Senate did not wish him to prosecute his campaign against Egypt—blunt words from over the sea. The king knew something of the Romans—not so much as he thought, but he was aware that the last king of Macedon had gone under. He said he would reflect upon his answer. Suddenly the Roman, who carried what the historians majestically call a staff but in ordinary language a mere walking-stick, drew a circle round the king as he stood, and said: "Answer me before you step out of that circle". The king thought for some moments and then said: "I will go back to Syria".

The three episodes tell our story in brief. We have what Virgil calls *populum regem*, a right royal senate of statesmen and world rulers, who by sheer weight of experience and character were better fit to rule the world than anybody in it at the time. Pyrrhus foresaw that the future of that people was not to be limited by Italy; and, one hundred years later, all the world, aghast at the abruptness and *gaucherie* of Popillius Laenas, recognized that, whoever might reign on the thrones of the Successors, Rome controlled all the lands of the Mediterranean. Some historians seem not to realize that there are two kinds of conquest, and that very often control is the most effective form of conquest; and Rome had achieved it. How had she done it?

This brings us at once to the Roman as the world saw him. He was a new type in the world. Alexander and his Successors had represented a type differing from the old Greek standards. This was a third kind of man, a variety unfamiliar, and not too welcome.

It is the legal mind in the soldier, the administrator, the supreme administrator who conquers and who keeps what he conquers. The Roman stood in marked contrast with the oriental monarchies who had to conquer and conquer again, who, at the beginning of each new reign, had to reduce the rebel states that revolted on the king's death, who never seemed able— apart from Darius—to organize and to hold what they won; in contrast, too, to the Successors of Alexander, who were, as we saw, subject to all the strange vagaries of Nature, degeneracy, the harem, and that curious survival of the unfittest, which haunts so many oriental monarchies. Here is a state, on the other hand, that endures, that never loses anything. Battles the Romans lost in plenty, sometimes campaigns, but their wars were apt to end in victory and Rome did not lose her provinces.

In brief summary, the work that the world saw the Roman do was this. Gradually he extended his power east and west, eastward over the old republics, leagues and monarchies, westward over the savage tribes of Gaul and Spain and Africa, and eventually, under the Emperors, over Britain. Rome was able to govern, to hold together, and to develop, all these varieties of men, different in race, in language, in temper, in civilization, by her political genius—if opportunism raised to the highest power can be called genius. The Romans were, says one of our historians, political opportunists to a degree unsurpassed in history. There was about them, for all their legal habit of mind, an elasticity, a pliability, an adaptability that surprises. There is no usage, cult or language of which they are intolerant, so long as it will fall in with the general scheme of things. Accept the position and keep your religion, keep your language, keep your laws; live as you will, but accept the Roman government. Rome is always able to raise armies, to send them here and there to the ends of the earth, to the Atlantic, to the Euphrates. She has amazing gifts in finance. She is able to meet immense expenses, civil and military. Hannibal and the Civil Wars must have strained her finances, and in the long run they broke down, but that was well on in the history of the Empire; and in the days of her growth she was never long hampered for money. It was also remarkable that Rome was able to trust her governors and her generals, as Athens never did with any ease of mind; Rome allowed them the very maximum of independence, with a certainty that they would do their work reasonably well. She trusted them and her trust was justified. Her conception of the magistrate centred in *Imperium*; he carried for the time the whole authority of the state. The word develops other suggestions, but remains Roman; it covers at last the world, the *Empire* as we call it derivatively, embracing in a universal order all that had been developed in the ancient world, bringing all the nations into one family. The idea became the foundation of all government, and was never lost; as it sank in political significance, it was reborn in a new sphere; the papacy rests on the old idea and reproduces the imperial system, still claiming to perpetuate the same unity of the world made Christian.[1]

[1] See Gregorovius, *History of the City of Rome in the Middle Ages*, vol. i, pp. 5, 6, 10, 12 (Engl. tr.).

To the Greek who really took the trouble to study him, the Roman was a very curious and interesting character. He thought in an utterly different way from all the familiar types of the world. He was frankly not interested in the things that absorbed the Greek. Political theory he never touched. As to philosophy, his attitude is traditionally shown by the story (possibly no more than a happy legend) of the proconsul, who came to the university town, summoned all the professors and told them that he understood there were points of dispute among them, but if they would come to his tribunal, he would settle them. Half the story, one might say, is repeated in Constantine, but only half; still it shows the Roman mind. The Roman was not at first interested in art. Polybius, at the sack of Corinth, saw Roman soldiers dicing, with a picture of Polygnotus for a table, a thing almost incredible for Greeks. It raises the old Greek question, the eternal question, which is the lower type, the man who knows not what he does or the man who deliberately does wrong? At first, the attitude of the Roman was contempt for all the supreme interests of Greece. Juvenal pictures the Roman soldier, when a town was taken, smashing the work of great artists, unconscious that it has any value.[1] The centurion in Persius will bid no more than a clipped shilling for one hundred philosophers. This early contempt for art and music, for painting and sculpture, is illustrated by the strange scene which Polybius records and which we may therefore take to be historical. There was a Roman who was to give a great national entertainment, and,

[1] Juvenal xi, 100 ff. *magnorum artificum frangebat pocula miles.*

misled by his Greek friend, included a contest of flute-players. To his horror, and to the disgust of the audience, it turned out to be something like a Welsh eisteddfod: the chagrin and boredom of host and audience were not to be fathomed. The adroit Greek went behind the stage and passed the word, and delight was restored when the two bodies of flute players advanced on one another and beat one another over the head with their flutes. What a people! and that story comes from Polybius, who knew and liked the Roman. After the ignorance that destroyed and despised, came the ignorance that collected, the horrible ignorance of the Roman collector, who pillaged and rifled the Greek cities where he went, carried away from temple and public square the things which the people had prized for generations, to decorate his dining-room.

That was one side of the Roman; and yet, on the other side, Strabo[1] speaks with interest of the curiously different ideals for a city that the Romans had. The Greek would adorn his city with statues and edifices of beauty; the Roman provided his city with a system of sewers. The French historian draws a contrast between the Greek navigator, with his eye upon the stars, making the discoveries on which rests the science of astronomy, and the Roman, building roads and setting up milestones; in the Greek world one tra-velled by the stars, in the Roman by the milestones. Professor Stuart Jones says that about 4000 Roman milestones have been found over the world. The earliest milestones known were those of Darius; the

[1] C. 235.

Hellenistic kings also set them up; but there was something about the milestone that went to the heart of the Roman; they were for him a passion—they were so sensible and practical, and to the Greek so needless and devoid of charm. Strabo further, in another passage,[1] remarks that the Roman had no real curiosity like the Greek. In fact, we may justly compare what the Greeks said and felt about the Romans with what Walter Bagehot wrote of another race; when he speaks of English character, he says that here the best people have no notion of play of mind, are characterized by a certain stiff dignity, by ignorance, and a clear want of flexible thought, and yet they have a rough sense of justice, they are generally fair-minded as free people are.[2]

On the whole the Roman in that Greek world is not unlike the Englishman in India to-day; not liked but trusted, a stupid type, very slow in the mind, not adroit, but in his slow way amazingly sensible in the long run, very capable, and surprisingly honest. The Roman, when they first met, startled the Greek with his honesty, as Polybius points out.[3] A Greek statesman, he says, entrusted with as much as a talent (£240), though there were ten checking clerks and no end of witnesses, is incapable of keeping his faith; while the Roman will handle thousands of talents in province or on campaign on the pledge of his word alone. It is a helpful type, amazing in its practical capacity, amazing in another way pointed out by Sir Richard Livingstone,[4] a nation that had no nerves, a

[1] C. 166. [2] Bagehot, *English Constitution*, pp. 93, 134.
[3] Polybius vi, 56. [4] *Classical Education*, p. 144.

nation with a genius for effective compromise, always ready very quickly to take the middle course. It is again a people, as Plutarch notes, meticulously careful in all that refers to ritual or the divine, in strange contrast to the slovenly ways of the Greek in handling his city's religion. Cicero emphasizes the same thing, and elsewhere speaks of the *naturalis quaedam prudentia* of the Italians, a certain common-sense given to the Italians by Nature herself.

Such was the people that was to rule the world. Behind their world destiny there is already a great national achievement, as Pyrrhus found, and Hannibal again, two generations later. Rome had united Italy; she had welded the Italians into one people, who, in spite of uncertainty here or there, perhaps, on the fringe, preferred their own flesh and blood to liberators from over the seas with Semitic features and foreign speech. Physical geography had not been against Rome as it was against Greece. Furthermore, the Italians were predominantly of one blood, on one level of culture. The Gauls in the north were below this level, as the Greeks in the south were above it; but it did not hurt Rome that the Gauls were below her in culture. At any rate, in those early years down to the invasion of Hannibal, she had really been doing in one land what Alexander meant to do for all the lands, and what Rome eventually did (in greater or less degree) all over the Mediterranean. The unification of Italy is a novel achievement in history, the making of a nation out of a country of independent clans and tribes.[1] The whole course of Roman political life had

[1] Perhaps Egypt might be quoted against me.

contributed to that movement for unification. Some readers may be amused, or even shocked, by the comparison of early Rome to early New York or New Amsterdam, in which, by the time it was twenty years old, a French Jesuit reports eighteen languages being spoken. Rome was a centre where from the beginning various races met, Aborigines (whatever they were; Dionysius so names them), Italians, Etruscans, Greeks, Carthaginians; the *plebs*, we must suppose, comprises them all, and their offspring of mingled blood. Here in one city, with some impossible compromises in government, duplicating consuls with tribunes, one assembly with another, both independent, there grows up a constitution which positively works, which welds into one community patrician, plebeian, Italian and stranger; and with it there is a remarkable growth of the constitutional intelligence and of the legal mind.

In an amazing passage in his *Laws*, Cicero tells us that, as a boy at school, like other boys in that day, though the practice had been given up by the time of his writing, he learned the XII Tables by heart, as a Greek boy would learn the *Iliad* and *Odyssey*, as Scottish boys used to learn the Catechism, and as English boys learn nothing.[1] Think for a moment of that astounding training; the boy with his mind steeped from childhood in legal principles, trained to think, not in Greek plays, not in books, not in philosophy, but in law; and he does think. There is some lack of

[1] In Finland quite recently children at school would learn the *Kalevala* by heart, some 20,000 lines; the national epic would create a national feeling. Perhaps Shakespeare serves our purpose in England.

imagination, as a result; but the training was surely justified by the men it made. Side by side with it went that parental Roman discipline, that brought the boy up to realize that he was a Roman, and was bound by his privileges. He lived to serve and to advance the commonwealth, by every form of self-sacrifice that the people and the Senate might call for; and for generations the son was true to his breed, lived the life and showed the spirit of father and grandfather.

There is nothing of this in the Orient so far as our records serve, or as we can deduce it from actual history; little enough of it in Greece. Law in the Orient was arbitrary; in Greece it was too fluid. The Greek was too individual to be the invariable patriot that the Roman was. I have sometimes thought that it is not quite idly that Aristotle fires his quip at the historians and tells us that history informs us what Alcibiades did and suffered. It is a quip: it is to support his thesis that "poetry is a more serious and philosophical thing than history"; but, after all, Alcibiades is in his way the typical Greek; and if one is asked the name of the typical Roman, it was probably Marcus. There have been people like Shakespeare and James Boswell in these islands, but the normal Englishman is John Doe or Richard Roe; and the Roman was Marcus; in both cases a monotonous but magnificent type.

There is a weakness in Roman conservatism which the Greeks at once saw, a weakness in the intellectual inertia of the people. In one of the most magnificent of Latin lines, Ennius says that the Roman community rests on character of the old type and men of the old type: *moribus antiquis stat res Romana virisque.* But how was the breed to be kept? The Roman father, and still more perhaps the Roman mother, at a certain stage, began to fail to produce that old character in the boys they brought into the world. The numbers of the family declined, and with the numbers the discipline. Perhaps from the first some impatience of thought and contrivance is betrayed by their government in their readiness to make shift with any arrangement that would serve for the time, in their habit of accommodation, in their refusal to re-think a constitution originally developed for a city-state, though now there was a widening world to be governed—all this in spite of their training in legal principle. Rome begins with the ordinary usage of the clan; settlement turns clan into canton, and then into city; and the system survives; and when first the nation grows and later the Empire, it has to serve as best it may, ludicrously unfit and outgrown as it was. The wonder is that it served so well, and the reason is to be found, as so often in English life, in the character of the men who work a system which in other hands must mean deadlock; "the Queen's government has to be carried on".

For, with all these drawbacks, with all its limitations and its weaknesses, the Roman type produced the senator, the soldier, the great proconsul. Edward Freeman said that the Roman Senate in its last century was still the salt of the earth, the last abiding place of freedom.[1] The Greeks were wondering whether it was chance or destiny, fluke or predestination, that ruled the world. In a magnificent passage Gibbon

[1] *Essays*, vol. ii, p. 337.

describes how "a wiser Greek deprived his country-men of this vain and delusive comfort by opening to their view the deep foundations of the greatness of Rome". Polybius told them that it was not by chance, it was not "automatically" (whatever that soothing word might mean),[1] that Rome had become mistress of the Mediterranean; it was reasonably to be expected from her character and her ways. The Roman put his mind on his work; he governed himself, and so he governed the world. He adopted the Spanish sword because it was the best sword for fighting purposes—the chief use after all of swords; and similarly he adapted means to ends, and changed army regulations and methods to meet real needs. Above all, there is that Roman character with its integrity, its amazing honesty, its devotion to the state, the application of practical reason and experience to all life.

Machiavelli in his *Prince*[2] says that the chief founda-tions of all states are good laws and good arms; and that might be the text of Polybius for his description of Rome in the great digression that makes his sixth book. We can sum up the story as the development of the legal mind, of political sense, of the instinct for government. Later on Roman character broke down, and government with it; but, in the meantime, Rome's rule of the world, as she gradually acquired it, had been essentially wise, and, in a hundred places of the Mediterranean, far better on the whole than what it replaced. Wherever it prevailed, it had meant, as Virgil says, peace and the spread of the arts of peace, civilization. Imperially the Roman is the heir

[1] Polybius i, 63, 9.   [2] *The Prince*, ch. 12.

of Alexander, as in many other ways he is the heir of the Greek in general.

There comes a period of disintegration and break-down, following, as Polybius says[1], the fall of the last Macedonian king, when it became quite clear to all the world from the action of Popillius Laenas, and to the Roman himself, that there was no further enemy for him to fear, that there was nothing standing be-tween him and universal empire. From this time onward Rome is invaded by Greeks often of a de-generate type, by oriental religion, by boundless wealth. Financial companies have growing power in politics. The influence of women and of freedmen increases. The homes are filled with slaves, men, women, and girls, white and often Greek, and clever enough as Roman comedy shows, some of them oriental and full of Asiatic superstition. Among them the young Roman has to grow up, and their ideas by natural process give a colour to his mind that is not Roman at all. Like the white child in India he is a *sahib* from the cradle, a sultan with a harem ready to hand. Roman religion was always strangely primitive, lacking the legend and mysticism that gave colour to Greek religion, and, like Greek religion, powerless to create and maintain conscience. It could give no support to the character, to the morals, on which, as Ennius said, the Roman commonwealth must rest. In Rome intellectual life, apart from law, was not native; it had to be imported from Greece; it was imitative, not widespread, nor generally instinctive. An unthought-out morality collapsed, as it always must.

[1] xxxii, 11.

There was no Socrates, no Plato, to show the foundations of morality, national and personal, in Nature,
until the Stoics began to find a foothold in the second
century; and they appealed to groups of intellectuals,
especially to the greater lawyers, rather than to society
at large. The political system, as we saw, had been
insincere for a century and a half, a collection of make-
believes and expedients, the adaptation of an outgrown theory to new conditions which it could not
cover. The Roman had been led on to the downward
slope of international aggression, and even Polybius
notes from time to time steps in diplomacy that at
best can only be called doubtfully moral. We watch
the rise of the army under the political adventurer,
the failure of reform, and then we see the city-state go
down, the republic disappear, in a black darkness of
materialism, mob rule and despair. The misery that
fills some of the intimate letters of Cicero is evidence
enough. Yet that there were still sound elements in
Rome is proved by the acceptance by Italy of a real
government under Caesar and Augustus. Cicero's is not
the last word in the story, as we shall see. The bad government was really human rather than Roman, and
was constantly countered by laws and courts, even if
ineffectually; and the Empire made amends for much.

But more relevant to our immediate purpose than
this failure of an outgrown republican system is the
higher life of Rome, and first of all the great development of law. "As boys", wrote Cicero, "we used to
learn the XII."[1] It is interesting to note the omission
of the noun. He learned the XII "as an inevitable

[1] Cicero, *de legibus*, ii, 23, 59.

jingle". Augustine speaks of the *odiosa cantio*, which you can hear outside a school, of the boys chanting "twice two is four, twice three is six". Then there came to Rome, as we saw, Greek philosophy, Stoicism; for we need say nothing at this point of Epicureanism. The Roman lawyer and the Greek Stoic had been made by God for one another. The Stoic brought with him two great conceptions embodied in two famous words; one of them he had found in the ordinary Greek vocabulary, and the other perhaps he coined for himself—nature and conscience (φύσις and συνεί-δησις). From the very formation of the XII Tables the Roman lawyer had been feeling his way to general principles of law, and, when he cast his eyes over a wider field than the civil law of Rome, he found the "law of races". It began simply enough in ordinary business; men of different tribes, races and cities became involved in litigation in a city like Rome where all races met; and the practical need of settlement drove the Roman lawyer to look into the laws of the various states concerned, and among them he found that certain types of law recurred; e.g. all states discouraged theft, murder, and adultery. Already practised in handling legal principle, he naturally brought it to bear on what he found, and he conceived of a law common to mankind. With this in his mind, he met the Stoic,[1] who also had thought deeply on these things, and still more upon Nature as the true basis of human life, and now suggested that behind the law of races lay the law of Nature. The state is no more fortuitous than man; it is no mere convention or agree-

---

[1] On Stoic influence see Maine, *Ancient Law*, ch. iii.

79

ment; it is natural. Man and the state are made by Nature, that was a Stoic dogma; and Nature has her laws, moral and physical, in obedience to which lies man's happiness and prosperity; to discover what those laws are, the Stoic habitually turned to what he called the consensus of mankind. Here was another phase of that consensus—the observed agreement among the laws of races. From this it was a natural and easy step to a greater conception of law than the Roman had reached—the law of Nature, that law of which one and another race has each something, scattered fragments, from the agreement of which the Roman had already framed his conception of the law of races. Nature has one law for all mankind. This conception consolidates all man's observation of natural processes, and gives a new basis for the development of natural science, as we call it. Taken in a sense rather different from what we usually give it, but cognate and germane, the conception at last dominates Roman law, and leads to changes of outlook, and to developments that humanize all legislation. The slave, for example, in old Roman law is one of several items to which the name *mancipium* is given, a class to be bought and sold by special and peculiar rules. In the law of all the nations he is an ordinary piece of property, like any other; the special class and the peculiar rules disappear; but still the slave is mere property. In the law of Nature there is no slavery. By Nature, says Ulpian, all men are born free. The Roman lawyer learnt it from the Stoics.[1]

---

[1] George Finlay, *History of Greece*, vol. iv, p. 45, emphasizes that the Byzantine Empire was hostile to slavery.

There is "a common law", then, for all mankind,
a κοινὸς νόμος as they call it[1]; and the Roman lawyers are inspired by the supreme influence of a great
central conception. In following it up, a new spirit
of critical inquiry is called forth, which involves new
developments of great significance in jurisprudence,
i.e. new outlooks, and wiser and more humane laws
as to slavery, marriage[2], and the state; a new desire
to get at the substance and the heart of things, to
find out the real meaning, the basic law of Nature,
and to secure that the law of the state came as near it
as possible. It pointed the way to a new equality, a
new freedom and a new recognition of the universal
human.[3] The supreme influence of a great central
conception slowly but surely transforming human life
is rarely to be so clearly seen; it is a very great contribution. Here we need not digress to corollaries—to
the new impulse to subordinate form to substance,
word to intention, which made the beginning of
Equity.[4] But we may urge that this new humanism
in Roman law and Roman thought surely recaptures
something of the mind of Alexander; and we may
anticipate what is to be said later and recall how
Prudentius says that for the coming of Christ the
Roman Empire was the preparation. That Roman
law with its Stoic background reacts, as Dean Merivale
pointed out,[5] upon religious ideas; it gives a philo-

[1] Arnold, *Roman Stoicism*, pp. 384, 385.
[2] W. W. Tarn, *Hellenistic Civilization*, p. 85.
[3] Lecky, *Morals*, vol. i, 297; with some remarkable quotations
from Roman lawyers on Nature, equality and freedom.
[4] Muirhead, *Roman Law*, p. 247.
[5] Merivale, *Conversion of Roman Empire*, p. 74.

sophic unity to all life, which naturally passed into
Christian thought. Roman law of this newer type,
a larger, more universal type, had much to do with
the shaping of Latin theology which was largely the
work of men trained in law and Stoicism.[1] The lawyer
was converted and became a Christian; he put his
gifts and his mind at the service of Christ, and he made
a clear contribution, for he thought now of his law of
Nature as the law of God. It is remarked by Lecky
himself that the renewed study of Roman law was an
important element in the revival that preceded the
Reformation. It was our thesis, set out in the first
chapter, that the Gospel had to win what was best in
the old world, and here it seems to be eminently
confirmed.

But Rome made other contributions to human
thought, and in the work of two of her sons we may
find the highest she gave. Perhaps few modern
Englishmen have a real admiration for Cicero. He
was a politician, and we do not greatly admire
politicians to-day; he was a statesman whose ideal was
in the past, and the present was sweeping it all away;
he was a stylist, and many of us are on our guard
where style is concerned. But, as one of the finest of
Oxford scholars has put it, "Style is thought", and
on reflexion there is a great deal in what Quintilian
says: "Let him know that he has made progress who
finds delight in Cicero".[2] Mommsen called Cicero a
"journalist". It is often true that a single sentence, a
single phrase, will exhibit a man's capacity for writing

[1] Tertullian and Cyprian, for instance; Tertullian is constantly
Stoic in his principles.   [2] Quintilian x, 1, 112.

history; one would hesitate to finish with Mommsen
for an epigram made in spleen, but it is a reminder
that a great historian may fail in sympathy, and so
failing may miss the real. At any rate this man,
various, quick, electric, was far cleverer than the
ordinary Roman; he was a humourist and therefore
suspect and the less to be trusted, the less likely to
reach in Rome, or in England, the highest places; and
he was, as Quintilian says,[1] "the supreme artist in
handling the minds of men". The art of writing letters,
it has been said, is reserved for those who have the gift
of friendship. No one wrote such letters as Cicero. He
was indeed a lover of men, a genuine lover of men.
"He loved young men," wrote Mr Warde Fowler,
"especially clever ones, and was apt to take an opti-
mistic view of them."[2] Could one think of anything
more engaging? And he adds: "There was no one of
that day of a humanity so real and so rare".[3] His life
and his letters make living a richer thing; they make
life better and finer; they suggest to you a charm about
the life that God has given to man to live—so greatly
does he enlarge your range, as you read him. He is a
believer in the state, and wrote much upon it. The
story is told of Augustus abruptly entering the room
where his grandsons were reading. They tried to hide
the book, but he picked it up and looked at it; it was
a volume of Cicero's letters; "he loved his country",
said the Emperor—a just verdict from an old opponent,
for which one must like him the better. Cicero, it is

---

[1] Quintilian xi, 1, 85.
[2] Warde Fowler, *Social Life in Rome*, p. 128.
[3] *Ib*. p. 112.

universally admitted, was a creator in language; he made Latin a tongue for philosophers, and gave ideals of grace to men of every other speech who study him. He had an exquisite sense of the beautiful in expression. Professor Rand of Harvard speaks of "the resonant and liturgical Latin of Cicero's *Dream of Scipio*".[1] There is a moral influence in great literature, whatever its theme; and it is indeed to be felt as you read Cicero. He is always the advocate of a higher life, a moral and reflective life, consciously and deliberately the advocate of it, and unconsciously, for his belief in the best informs all he does. With all his weaknesses, says Mr Heitland, there hangs about him "a certain atmosphere of truth, of goodness and of nobility".[2] He was the most highly cultivated man of antiquity, says Mr Warde Fowler. He loved all that was beautiful—a beautiful house, works of art, poetry. He dreamed that he could write verse, and Juvenal laughed at him for it, but Virgil read Cicero's verse and learned something. If he was no poet, he certainly could write prose.

In his personal ideals and endeavours, far more than in his successes, Cicero sets conscience on the throne of life. He was the Latin world's teacher in philosophy. St Augustine, in his *Confessions*,[3] tells us that, as a young man, he happened upon Cicero's book called *Hortensius* and that this book changed his ambitions, his desires, his mind, his whole outlook upon life. Such a passage gives us some measure of the reality of Cicero's service to mankind. The man is not

[1] E. K. Rand, *Founders of the Middle Ages*, p. 266.
[2] W. E. Heitland, *The Roman Republic*, § 1345.
[3] *Confessions*, iii, 47.

to be despised who can capture an Augustine. For Augustine is still one of the greatest minds the world has yet seen; he is still a living influence and will be while Christianity lasts and Latin is read; and he was won over to the higher life by a book of Cicero; and, we are told, he never forgot his debt to Cicero;[1] nor was he the only one of the Fathers who owed such a debt. Rand emphasizes Cicero's contribution to the interpenetration of Christian theology with Greek philosophy.[2] It was through Cicero that Greek thought reached the world. "Mere copies", he writes to Atticus of his philosophic works: "all I supply is the words—and I have plenty of them"; and the odd thing is that so many readers should have taken the playful self-depreciation of an intimate letter so solemnly; perhaps they do not understand a serious man laughing at himself in talk with a friend who understood his talk and liked it. In any case, Cicero loved philosophy; and, however much he drew from the books of Greeks earlier or later, there is a certain original value in his own work. It was the first time that a real man of affairs, a statesman of the first rank, trained in national life and in international life, put his mind to Greek philosophy. He was also the first foreigner of ability to criticize the conclusions of Greek philosophers and the principles of Greek thought. Both these facts have a value, which the doctrinaire may very readily miss. Granted that he translates from Posidonius, it is a contribution to thought to know what impressed such a man as Cicero; he gives a

[1] Gibb and Montgomery, intr. to Aug. *Conf*. p. xix.
[2] E. K. Rand, *Founders of the Middle Ages*, p. 52.

85

stamp to what he takes. There is an originality in criticism, in selection. Genius has been called the instinct for the significant fact; and Cicero had it. The world was very content to lose the books of Posidonius, but it kept Cicero, to play once more a significant part in the Renaissance and the formation of European culture.

A few words about Virgil shall end our chapter— *Romanus Vergilius*, Italian and Roman, the first great poet, I think, who ever interpreted a country, deliberately knowing what he was doing for his people, in sheer love of his land. Whatever else they are, the *Georgics* were a revelation of Italy. Italy in those days was, to every cultured person, as prosaic and humdrum as the newer part of Canada is to-day to old world exquisites; and Virgil saw the land as such men did not in his day—the beauty of the scene, the ancient hill-top towns, *fluminaque antiquos subterlabentia muros*, the worth of the race, *patiens operum parvoque adsueta juventus*. The *Aeneid* has been called *Gesta Populi Romani*, "the acts of the Roman people"; it is the greatest of his works, which grows upon you if you will read it, as he wrote it, in one piece. Virgil, wrote Robert Louis Stevenson,[1] "is one of the tops of human achievement"; he is "stricken down with admiration". Full of Italian scene, of religious ritual, of antiquarianism, the *Aeneid* is not the book the schoolboy supposes; and many have nothing beyond a schoolboy knowledge of it. Let its framework be Homeric, its legend impossible, out of it come three things: the worth once more of that Italian race, the value of

[1] Letter to Colvin, March 1886; and again December 1887.

human character as seen in Aeneas, and of the
Imperium that God has given to the Roman people.
Moderns have laughed at his hero; let them! He is
a hero of a new type, a man of large range, wide in
outlook, tender in heart, a man with a mission, for
whom it is a necessity to have life related to heaven.
Virgil, "lord of language", founded an immortal
tradition in poetry. Apart from form and word, and
in them, he trained the finest feeling of his people, and
their imagination, as we see once more in Augustine,
who wept for Dido and *ipsius umbra Creusae*.[1] And
perhaps his influence was, and remains, the greater,
because there is in Virgil that ancient quarrel of
poetry and philosophy, of which Plato speaks.[2] I
would ask the question: Must that quarrel ever be
present, that war ever be waged, in all the greatest of
human hearts? I rather think so. Virgil also is
making the world into which the Gospel comes; and
with him Christ has to reckon. Let the chapter end
with the splendid sentence of Sainte-Beuve: "The
coming of Jesus Christ has nothing to astonish when
one has read Virgil".

[1] Augustine, *Conf.* i, 13, 22.
[2] Plato, *Republic*, 607 A.

V

THE JEW

Of all figures in the old Mediterranean world, the strangest and the most enigmatic alike to his fellow-subjects and to the modern student of history is the Jew. Even then in the great cities he was what we find him in the great centres of to-day—an alien, well established but the readiest of men to emigrate in search of business, holding himself aloof from the rest of mankind and dissatisfied with their retaliation of exclusiveness, repulsive to the Western in his habits, repellent in spirit, sharing fitfully in the world's culture but always foreign to it. He was indeed a perplexing figure; was it race or religion that prevented him alone of all men from amalgamation with the rest of mankind? Why should his god alone among gods insist on haughty isolation from Olympus, where were gathering gladly enough the gods of all the peoples, as we see in their dedications and other religious inscriptions, and in the gay mockery of Lucian? Like the Druid, whom he did not otherwise resemble in the least, it might be said of the Jew that he alone knew or alone was ignorant of the gods. Why would the Jew not inter-marry with other races? Why would he not eat with them? Why would he insist on one idle day in every seven? Why circumcision? Why his eternal fussiness (ψοφοδεές) about obviously wholesome food? Bacon, for instance, was a perfectly religious diet, as Plutarch's father maintained. All these points of difference were at once obvious, and to the common man ludicrous; and ludicrous they remain to the common man, who accepts to this day the taboos of the Jew's heathen contemporaries as natural and proper—the virginity taboo, the celibacy of clergy, fasting, and the refusal of horse-flesh, not one of them in essence less absurd than the Jew's refusals.

The answer to all these questions is to be sought in history; but Greeks were little interested, apart from such rare spirits as Herodotus and Xenophon, in the history or literature of foreigners. Polybius, as we have seen, complained of Greek inattention to the conquering Roman, whom the Greek historians were content to ignore or leave uninterpreted. Berossus and Manetho are regarded by the modern students of their fragments as masters in carelessness and inaccuracy. How little the Romans knew or cared to know about Jewish history is shown by the famous introduction set by Tacitus in the front of the fifth book of his *Histories*. Yet Josephus was almost his contemporary and in the circle of Vespasian, and took infinite pains to familiarize any one who would read Greek with the Jew's apologies for his existence and his beliefs.

The clue to the Jew's mind lies of course in his history; and there is this defence at least available for the careless Greek or Roman, that the history of the Jew is to this day almost beyond our ascertaining. True, the Old Testament is to be read in hundreds of languages, and it presents a sort of authorized version of Jewish history. For the Jew, like the rest of us (the Hindu excepted), enjoyed the study of his antecedents, thought over his history, wrote it and rewrote it, and the outcome is in the Old Testament. But to the modern student history rewritten is not history more lucid. Modern study of anthropology, modern archaeological discoveries in the soil of Palestine, of Egypt and Babylonia, have brought much to light—a mass of buried fact which is hard to reconcile with the ancient Jew's theory of what Hebrew history had been; many questions have been raised, and the answers are almost as perplexing as the problems. "As I practised conjecture more", wrote Samuel Johnson of his Shakespearean studies, "I learned to trust it less"; and his sentence will recur to those who read the ancient history of the Jews as written to-day. This is not to reject the abundance of facts that the diligence of research has produced, but to express the uneasiness of a historical student at the reconstructions attempted. To learn that history, we have to study the Old Testament narrative, as it stands, in relation to what it perhaps was before Jewish redactors adjusted its data to their theories; and then to harmonize our results with the boundless detail given us from the histories and literatures of Egypt and Mesopotamia, and lastly with the revelations of the spade in one or another centre of civilization and worship in Palestine.

The great figures of the ancient history of Israel are familiar to us—some of them too familiar, so well cloaked in legend do they come to us. Moses is allowed to-day, by grace of modern historians, to return from limbo to the historical scene; but it wakens some doubts to find the same group of authorities sending back Agamemnon with him. Elijah stands more securely

within the historical area, but he would be a bold man
who would write Elijah's history. Perhaps as illumi-
nating an instance as any of the welding of history and
legend, is Solomon. Few stories in the Old Testament
or elsewhere are so vivid as that of the adventures of
David, few so dull as that of the glories of Solomon.
Everything about the wise king is overlaid with gold
and splendour and incredible arithmetic. One fact of
real significance seems to slide in amid the magnifi-
cence, but its value is generally lost to the reader,
though it may explain much of what follows. He
appears to have tried, like the French revolutionists,
to regroup his people on a new basis, and to substitute
administrative areas for the old tribes;[1] but the tribes
were too much for him and his son. The story of the
queen of Sheba plays a large part in ancient legend,
though it can perhaps only have been after Ethiopia
(as we are now to call Abyssinia) became Christian
that its kings claimed descent from Solomon and his
splendid visitor. Over all hangs somehow, like a mist,
the king's repute for unexampled wisdom, which
must assuredly have some origin, not revealed by
anything beyond one decision embodied in a tale of
a popular type. The *Proverbs* and the *Wisdom* of
Solomon, like his *Odes*, belong to a much later period,
when his fame was strong enough to float an entire
literature. Out of the clouds emerge some very
definitely historical figures, the incomparable David,
the two Jeroboams, and Ahab always interesting. But
the two men of the Old Testament who are to be
known most intimately are Jeremiah and Nehemiah,

[1] A. Bertholet, *Hebrew Civilization* (Engl. tr.), p. 243.

standing at the end of the older period and the beginning of the newer, with a dim century and a half
between them; they at least have personality and
character, to be read in their own writings—natures
intelligible, sympathetic, human and individual beyond all others of Jewish story.

Of history in our modern sense of the word we have
little enough. The Jews were convinced that their
ancestors went to Egypt, were enslaved, were delivered, and were led to Palestine. So much may in
general be true, but the detail of the story is beyond
us; no man now can unravel (unless it be to his own
satisfaction) the relations of the tribes of Israel and
their ancestors and gods. Was Gad a son of Jacob or a
god? Was Joseph a vizier of Egypt, or a "Hebrew"
tribe long before in Palestine, or something else?
Once in Palestine, what did they do with the people
they found there? *Deuteronomy*, the oldest canonical
book (some say), enacts the killing of the Canaanites,
but it is suggested that this was to explain their disappearance. "Their heads are gone, if it please your
Majesty!" say the soldiers in a modern tale. Hebrew
history left men supposing that Hittites and Hivites
were much of a muchness; archaeology reveals that
the Hittites were an imperial people with wide
dominions and a great foreign office, not a mere local
clan. Other questions arise as to the influence of
Canaan and its tribes and local Baals, of the greater
nations, Egyptian and Assyrian, Babylonian and
Persian—questions not easily answered.

Happily, for our present purpose, it is not necessary
to rewrite the history of Israel, significant as it was for

the emergence somehow of a unique type of religion.
We cannot even write the history of that religion. God
spoke to Abraham and Moses, we read in the books
of the Hebrews; He did not exactly speak to them,
because perhaps they were tribes or eponymous
figures or legends, we have since been told, but somehow or other——. "Somehow or other" is not satisfac-
tory history; the one version is as inexplicable as the
other, the modern reconstruction as the Jewish.
Enough, that after a welter of reigns and rebellions,
one captivity or two or more of the whole or a
part of the people, after the undoubted activity of a
series of prophets, real figures if less luminous than
Jeremiah, we have a "Return", full again of per-
plexities for the modern student. Not many in reality
did return; "the bulk of the captivity remained in
Babylon and considered themselves the pick of
Judaism".[1] But from this period we can speak of the
Jewish religion.

Nehemiah belongs to the reign of Artaxerxes, and
is roughly dated about 450 B.C. It was revealed
about 1906 by the chance discovery in Egypt of the
Sachau papyrus that in 410 B.C. Egyptians, moved by
religious or tribal hate, destroyed a Jewish temple at
Yeb or Elephantine (two names for one town) which
Cambyses a century before had spared. A Jewish
temple in Egypt clashed with all we had ever read in
Deuteronomy, but there it was—a witness to our
ignorance of real Hebrew history and to our depend-
ence on reconstructions of it contrived by Jews after
the period of Ezra, a tremendous if very dim figure,

[1] Elkan Adler, in *Judaism and the Beginnings of Christianity*, p. 97.

who for the Jews overshadowed the more attractive or at least better known Nehemiah.

Roughly two centuries after Nehemiah the Old Testament was translated into Greek in Egypt. Wonderful legends gathered about this translation; it became a thing of miracle; while a few centuries later another kind of legend and miracle attended it— a plague of darkness hung over Palestine while it was making; it became an alien book, the text-book of the great enemy. Meanwhile it is a landmark of the highest importance. It implies something like a canon of scripture—with some uncertainty of margin, it is true. It shows us the Jew in a new environment, with a new language, thinking new thoughts, in the new world that Alexander made.

Once more, as ancient story told of his early days in Canaan, the Jew began by feeling the attraction of the new environment. A Jewish historian tells how Jason practically bought the High Priesthood from Antiochus Epiphanes for some hundreds of talents, and how he used his power.[1] The inhabitants of Jerusalem were to be registered as citizens of Antioch and brought over to Greek ways of life. Former royal concessions to the Jews were discarded, and the High Priest "brought in new customs forbidden by the law. For he eagerly established a Greek place of exercise under the citadel itself, and caused the noblest of the young men to wear the broad Greek hat (*petasos*). And thus there was an

[1] *Maccabees*, iv, 7–17. The hat is more significant than a mere modern fashion. Bombay has sixty varieties of turban, all indicating differences of race, place and religion, and pictured in the *Gazetteer*. This was before Mr Gandhi's hat came into fashion.

extreme of Greek fashions and an advance of an alien
religion, by reason of the extreme profaneness of Jason,
that ungodly man and no high priest, so that the
priests had no more any zeal for the services of the
altar; but, despising the sanctuary and neglecting the
sacrifices, they hastened to enjoy that which was un-
lawfully provided in the palaestra, after the summons
of the discus; making of no account the honours of
their fathers and thinking the glories of the Greeks best
of all". Such was the appeal of the external features
of Hellenism. The story of "the attempt of Antiochus
Epiphanes to abolish superstition, to introduce Greek
ways, and thus to reform a detestable race",[1] and how
it was frustrated by a Parthian War and by the spirit of
the Maccabees, is familiar. Yet the king, says a modern
Jew, was less the promoter than the instrument of the
policy which had its roots in the corruption of a part
of the Jewish people.[2] The episode, the clash, the
deliverance, made one thing certain; Judaism was not
to be lost in an amalgam of races and religions;
particularism triumphed, and mankind may be glad
that it did. Two comments may be made before we
pass on to larger and nobler aspects of the meeting of
Jew and Greek. With the Jew as with the Greek, it is
not to the Temple that we must look for real progress
in religion. Jeremiah long before had insisted that
Jehovah was independent of any local structure in
Jerusalem. A religion that has no idol to house, says
G. F. Moore, has no real need of a temple.[3] That this

[1] Tacitus, *Histories*, v, 8.
[2] N. Bentwich, *Hellenism*, p. 93.
[3] G. F. Moore, *Judaism*, vol. i, p. 26.

is so, is proved by what followed the final destruction of the Temple by Titus in A.D. 70. Judaism, bitterly as patriot Jews may have lamented the fall of city and shrine, was freed from an incubus, which, whatever may have been true in "Deuteronomic" days, had no shred of spiritual value. The hereditary priesthood, Sadducees in both meanings of the word, original and derivative, had surrendered to Antiochus and idolatry; they compromised with Rome; they accepted Herod's Temple, and they resisted every forward movement in religious thought. Strabo hints that they were hand and glove with bandits and brigands, and, whatever he means, whether he refers to rights of asylum making the Temple a den of thieves or to patriot bands (like modern Greek *Klephts*), the suggestion is unpleasant and hardly implies spiritual leadership. A further comment may seem an idle speculation, since the attempt of Antiochus failed and the Temple was rededicated after three years of pollution on 25 December 164;[1] but would the complete conversion of Jerusalem and the Temple to Greek idolatry have affected the belief, as opposed to the sentiment, of the greater Jewish community throughout the world? That the destruction of both by Titus increased the power and significance of the synagogue, is the verdict of historians; would their earlier passing have meant much else? But it is idle to speculate upon the possible consequences of what did not happen.

The distinctive contribution of the Jewish people to the ancient world, and to humanity, is a type of religion, essentially unexampled elsewhere. The origins

[1] E. R. Bevan, in *Cambridge Ancient History*, vol. viii, p. 515.

of that religion it seems idle, and irresistible, to explore, as we have suggested. We are not likely to have much clear evidence added to explain the source or the meaning of the name *Yahweh*, to enlighten us as to the earliest conceptions the Hebrews accepted or framed to interpret their peculiar god. The outlines of the progress of the people from polytheism to the sole supremacy and then to the sole existence of their God, we can make out in the Old Testament; but much is hidden and seems likely to remain hidden. Egypt and Persia had great religious movements; Akhenaton (Amenophis IV)[1] and Zoroaster are both profoundly interesting; but it is difficult to determine the influence of either upon Hebrew thought, and indeed not specially important. The religious reformer of Egypt failed to influence his people; Zoroaster's faith has been overthrown and almost extinguished by the adherents of a religion largely Jewish in origin; Judaism still lives. After all it is the thing that lives that is important; what it assimilates is interesting, but less interesting than the conquering faith. And in that pre-Christian age Judaism conquered; it rose above all its rivals; whatever it assimilated, it remained true to itself; it inspired a people still significant in every civilized land; it challenged the ancient world and made contributions still unexhausted to all mankind. The Greek is far more relevant to the story than Babylonian or Persian, if for nothing else, because he compelled the Jew, as later on he compelled the Christian, to think out to its depths what his religion really meant.

[1] See Adolf Erman, *Egyptian Religion*, p. 62 f.

The very fact that the Old Testament was translated, and had to be translated, into Greek, is a historical fact of the greatest importance. It was not made by a Luther or by a modern missionary to secure a change in national or tribal thinking; it was made because a race had changed its language and wished to understand its religious faith. At least the wide and quick acceptance of the version suggests so much, whatever the part played by unknown pioneers of translation or by King Ptolemy himself—if he played any part at all. It is significant, however, that the translators, whether working as a group or as individuals, in spite of natural tendencies to literalism and to the use of Hebraisms—the failings of all translators—here and there avoided renderings too literal of phrases congenial in another age and another language. The Almighty is not called a "Rock"; "Lord" is substituted for the sacred name;[1] the anthropomorphisms are toned down; God does not repent, is not seen, has not a hand.[2] It is not common for a translator to achieve a beauty of style beyond his author; more usually the version falls short of the original; and those who commend the Septuagint to us have but qualified praise for its language or music. It reads more happily in narrative passages, as one might expect, than in prophetic or lyric. But all this is aside from our point, which is that the version was

[1] It is a very curious phenomenon that the American "Standard" version should force back the hands of the clock to a date earlier than 280 B.C. by restoring the word *Jehovah* (invented in the fifteenth century A.D.) in place of "the LORD"—a remarkable triumph of pedantry over religious insight.

[2] See Drummond, *Philo Judaeus*, i, 158.

needed, was called for, was accepted, and had untold influence in the religious development of mankind. It is a monument of the meeting of the races, a landmark in the movement towards Alexander's ideals.

Greek influence upon Jewish life and thought meets us everywhere. It has been calculated, we are told, that there are three thousand borrowed words, mostly Greek, in the Talmud—official and legal terms, names of plants and animals naturally enough, terms to convey abstract and scientific ideas, where Greek would seem inevitable in every language, and even νόμος for the Torah.[1] It is curious to find Josephus, the great apologist for his people to the Greek world, owning that he never mastered Greek pronunciation.[2] Palestine was invaded by the musical instruments of the Greek, citharis, psaltery, the *symphonia* (the favourite instrument of Epiphanes and perhaps mentioned in the story of the Prodigal Son). The well-known *Selah* of the Psalms has been explained, rightly or wrongly, as a Greek musical term—ψάλλε, strike the harp. Outside Palestine Jewish interest in the theatre is proved by the discovery of an inscription reserving seats for Jews in the theatre at Miletus, and by a psychological observation of Philo as to changes of mood in an audience. St Paul's metaphors betray an early acquaintance with athletics; his life has been a good contest, he has made a race of it, and (it would seem) kept his torch burning, and the Judge has a crown for him.[3] As we have seen already, the so-

---

[1] N. Bentwich, *Hellenism*, p. 306.
[2] Josephus, *Antt.* xx, 263. [3] Cf. chapter vii, p. 146.

called Wisdom Literature, if it begins by being thoroughly Hebrew, proverbial and prudential, moves on to thoughts of the First Author of beauty, of the cosmos, and of immortality—"the souls of the righteous are in the hand of God". It might be too abrupt to attribute interest in immortality exclusively to Greek influence, but it is remarkable how little mention of it there is in the canonical scriptures, late as some of them are. The writer of *Ecclesiastes*, the only pleasant book according to Renan that a Jew has written, is generally recognized as a cultured Jew acquainted with Greek philosophy, genially cynical, a disbeliever in immortality as he takes pains to emphasize; and his book slipped into the canon in virtue perhaps of moral saws with which he decorated it for the unsuspecting, or which some interpolator—— but there are too many interpolators in the critical schools of Greece and Judaea alike; perhaps it was his adroitness in attributing his work to the all-wise King Solomon. Ezekiel, not the prophet, is a poet, known to us in fragments quoted by Eusebius from his Greek tragedy on the Exodus. Dr Rendel Harris has found traces of another tragic poet in the story of the Ptolemaic persecution of the Jews. Strangest of all, the Sibyl or Sibyls of Greek legend were inspired by Jewish theology, and made, in Greek hexameters with a philosophic tinge, prophecies of the triumph of religion.

All the Greek world talked philosophy or listened to it, till it became almost inevitable for a man who thought at all to think in Greek terms original or translated, or at all events along Greek lines. Cicero and Marcus Aurelius are Romans, practical to the core, but each is a thinker and goes to Greece for his language and method of thought. Paul was no philosopher; he was untrained (he says, and it is clear) in Greek culture; but he lived among Greeks, he liked them and understood them, and, outsider as he was, he must use the great Stoic words Nature and Conscience; a man who studied the *Wisdom of Solomon* and lived in Tarsus could hardly speak otherwise. Outstanding above them all is Philo, "the Jew", as he is called, but his significance is far greater in Christian than in Jewish literature, as the *Logos* doctrine must remind us. "Few, if any", writes Dr Theodore Robinson, "have ever understood or expounded Plato better, and yet his primary interest was to expound Moses."[1] He stands for the verbal inspiration of the Old Testament, but by his theory of allegory "turns it into a moral and metaphysical romance"— the method of the Greek mysteries, he calls it. "To comprehend God, we must first become God, which is impossible"; we can only *know* that God *is*; but he takes refuge in Platonic ideas, and gives God character, so far as man can, by finding their archetypes in God. God's work, in a more or less Platonic way, is delegated to "Powers", ideas in action, *Logoi*, all summed up in the *Logos*, eternal archetype and eternal activity, but not personal.[2] In his use of allegory, a use he shared with Stoic interpreters of Homer, he gave Christian scholars of Alexandria a hint they were quick to take; and in much else he was their pioneer; he gave them

[1] *Hebrew Religion*, p. 341.
[2] See W. R. Inge, *Plotinus*, vol. i, pp. 97–99.

a philosophic language and approach, and he taught them to think on Greek lines. It is arguable that they need not have followed him as loyally as they did, that they did too much reconciling on his lines of the thought of Jesus with the doctrines of Plato, but that lies outside our present theme.

On the other side there were Jews who were little interested in Hellenism or influenced by it; and to them we must attribute the apocalyptic literature, which of late has had an attention out of all proportion to its merits, a mass of chaotic books, bad enough to start with, and made worse by interpolation of matter as bad. Taste and language and spirit are all wrong together; and yet the writers do not escape from their day and its influence. They have to face the questions of immortality and retribution; they have to find some kind of rhythm or reason in history; so far Roman or Herodian oppression, or the times generally out of joint, compel them to think; and, despite their nationalism and their dreary use of dull parable, something Greek, something philosophic, finds its way into their minds and their books.

Jewish influence upon the Gentile world is harder to trace, but it is to be found. The Greeks and the Romans wrote no literature of conversion; it is only in stray fragments of Christian biography that we come upon our evidence—and in the indignation or amusement of a Juvenal, a Celsus or a Horace. Longinus indeed cites as an example of the sublime the sentence of "the legislator of the Jews, no ordinary man"— "God said, Let there be light and there was light"; but such interest in foreign writers is rare among Greek readers, if not unexampled.[1] The Jews were every-where; Josephus quotes Strabo to the effect that they are in every city, and that it is hard to find a place in the habitable earth where this tribe is not. They were expelled from Rome in 139 B.C., and returned, to amuse Horace, to be expelled by Claudius and to half-convert Poppaea Sabina; *in qua te quaero proseucha?* Whatever other racial groups may have done as to living in quarters by themselves, as in modern New York, there is evidence that in many places the Jews lived apart. In its original institution this may have been a con-cession to be associated with their special privileges as an *ethnos*. Gentiles in modern times have always pre-ferred not to live in a quarter where the Jews are; and whether they confined the Jew to a particular area, or left it when he came in, whether he preferred it (as is probable) or not, he had it to himself. The Jewish community was known as *diaspora* or *paroikia* (parish); and they had certain privileges conceded by Julius Caesar—of self-government, of synagogue rule, of exemption, to some extent, from army service, beside a special concession that they were not to be brought before ordinary law courts on a Saturday.

Their Sabbath and their superstitions called atten-tion to them; and, whatever satirists might say, the prudent legislator recognized what he could not alter, where it did no obvious harm. Their religion was "licensed"—a *religio licita*, a *vectigalis libertas*. Their synagogues were all over the world, even in Athens. In the Piraeus one would have expected to find a synagogue; Dr Verrall even looked for one in the days

[1] Longinus 9, 9.

of Aristophanes, rather prematurely.[1] In Athens, too, strange as it ought to seem, Stoics and Epicureans are willing, or even wishful, to listen to the Jew from Tarsus, untrained in Greek culture as he is and foreign of accent. It is very significant. In the synagogue the Jew learned to do without the Temple. The victory of the Jerusalem monopolist killed the old religion. Priest, altar, sacrifice, and ritual, if they could only be had in Jerusalem, must be foregone, and in Babylon and Alexandria Jews learnt the surprising lesson that religion is independent of all these things, which they had once, like the heathen still, counted indispensable. The New Testament is our chief source of knowledge of the synagogue in its earlier centuries, and it is confirmed by Josephus.[2] When the Christians seceded or were expelled, they repeated the order of service in their new room with a new emphasis—readings from the Old Testament, exposition, prayer and hymn. This was not old-time religion, but the synagogue had found it of value; and the destruction of the Temple showed it was more valuable even than men had supposed. Others beside Jews learnt the value of synagogue worship.

From time to time we have seen in glimpses movement in Greek religious thought—a demand for something more intellectual, more thinkable, more intelligent, than open temple ceremony or the mysteries offered, something moral and free from magic and nonsense. Alexander, as we saw, drove men to seek

[1] Orontes, however, says W. W. Tarn, *Hell. Civil.* p. 89, flowed into Ilissus before it flowed into Tiber.
[2] Cf. Josephus, *c. Apionem*, ii, 17, 175.

a universal religion, a universal god—One God, we might almost say. In the synagogue men found something very closely akin to what they were seeking. Here was spiritual worship, dependent on mind and heart rather than ritual or sacred formula. There was no magic in the synagogue; all was open; the appeal was to thought, not to mysterious terror. Religion, again, was here in closest association with pure morals and high conduct[1]—a Platonic requirement which the Greek and Roman temples never dreamed of asking. The religion was monotheistic—and the immense appeal of this is seen in the words of Tatian, of Justin, of the Christian apologists; to be set free once and for all from a myriad of half-devil gods, and to have to do with One God, all-wise and all-righteous, meant sanity and happiness. To Aristotle it seemed odd to talk of "loving a god"; in the Psalms, sung in the synagogue, religion found an emotional centre in *loving* the One God.

How far this appeal reached, we do not know. We have no religious statistics for the ancient world, a fact often forgotten by those who write on the mystery cults. We are told by modern Jewish writers of thousands of converts; Gibbon suggested that the number of proselytes was never much superior to that of apostates; the evidence seems difficult to find. Isis perhaps drew to herself more adherents; she asked for no circumcision; and her ritual was more impressive to the shallow-minded and (it is suggested sardonically by Christian writers) more expensive. But in the *Acts of the Apostles*, in the story of Paul's travels, we find the

[1] Cf. Josephus, *c. Apionem*, ii, 22, 190 ff.; 24, 202, no infanticide.

circle of adherents round every synagogue, ready to listen, readier than the Jews; and it is hardly guess-work to conjecture that it was among the proselytes of one degree or another that the Christian apostle found his first converts, and when they were won, the door was open for direct work among the Gentiles; the synagogue was needed no more, and it became a focus of bitter opposition. Judaism swung away from Hellenism in anger not yet forgotten. The proselytes, bag and baggage, went to the Christian church and were welcome to go; and the hellenizing Jews went with them.[1] The Septuagint was repudiated and execrated; its very making was comparable with the making of the golden calf; a fast day was appointed to mark the calamity. Greek culture was banished from Jewish schools from the end of the second century.[2] The Christian Gospel and King Antiochus make a strange pair, but they provoked a similar reaction.

But meanwhile Judaism had done the world service, unconsciously carrying out the ideas of Alexander and preparing the way for a yet larger unity of mankind.

[1] Bentwich, *Hellenism*, p. 301.   [2] *Ib*. pp. 287 ff.

THE ROMAN EMPIRE

To attempt to deal with so vast a subject as the Roman
Empire in the compass of a short chapter has something absurd about it. But to understand the New
Testament some acquaintance with the central conceptions that make that Empire, if not with its detail,
is imperative. The object proposed in these pages is not
so much to outline a system as to give some feeling for
what the Empire meant, what it did to legitimate
itself, what spirit animated those charged with the care
of it, and to argue that it was not, as some people have
lightly thought, a tyranny, a curse to mankind, but a
forward movement and a blessing.[1] It would not be
untrue to say that Rome was the heir of Alexander's
empire and of Alexander's ideas. What the King conceived, what the King tried to do, what the King
partly did and had to leave half done to the Successors,
who did not wholly carry out his purpose or his ideas
nor wholly abandon them, the Republic in the west
achieved. Little by little, at first certainly with no
idea of her destiny, Rome spread her power over the
Mediterranean, till at last she united the whole
Mediterranean world under one control, and then

[1] The phrase is almost that of Polybius i, 4, 4: Rome's power—
"the most beautiful and beneficent device of Fortune (*Tyche*)".
Whatever he eventually meant by *Tyche*, he found reason (as we
saw) in Rome's rule, and the rest of his phrase stands.

gradually, as need from time to time required, she brought it under one administration. For long semi-independent kingdoms, protected principalities, were allowed to continue; but in time, in the Roman phrase, first the Senate, later the Emperors, reduced each of the kingdoms to the form of a province. Rome, one may say, re-established the empire of Alexander, limiting it wisely at the Euphrates eastward, but with a wider sway to the west, and a stronger hold, and very largely achieved that unity of the world of which the great King had dreamed. In all her work in the eastern Mediterranean there is a certain continuity with that of the houses of Seleucus and Ptolemy. She did assuredly preserve and diffuse Hellenism; Asia Minor became far more definitely Greek under her rule, and Greek it remained till the great transportations of 1922, which left it less Greek than it was in the days of Homer, and less Christian than in the days of St Paul. Westward Rome's work of hellenization has been more lasting; and perhaps it was not a drawback that the medium was the Latin language.

It may be fairly urged that Rome's title was in the main legitimate. Livy, in an interesting sentence,[1] says that Rome "extended her sway almost more by sparing the conquered than by conquering". Perhaps he was thinking of a famous line of Virgil. A very remarkable survey of the world is given by Strabo, writing in the time of our Lord; "no more picturesque book remains", says Mr Tarn,[2] "since Herodotus". In an interesting paragraph[3] Strabo tells his Greek readers

[1] xxx, 42.　　　　　　　　[2] W. W. Tarn, *Hellen. Civil.* p. 236.
[3] Strabo, C. 127.

that Rome has taken under her sway many races by nature uncivilized because of their geographical situation, the mountains they inhabited, their harbourless lands, the cold of their climate, their distance from other races and from culture; and, adding them to her Empire, she has interwoven the civilized and the uncivilized and has taught the wilder peoples to live the life of citizens—he uses the word significant to a Greek, *politicôs*. Thus, he continues, both types of land and people contribute and receive benefits; the rougher and stouter breeds supply armies and soldiers; the more favoured races contribute products of the soil, the arts, and all that makes character; and now under the Roman Empire, he says, the peace-loving elements predominate. The Romans, he concludes, in this work carry on what Greek and Macedonian began. That is a passage to make any one think, and the ancients did think about the Roman world, as we shall see. We have to remember that hellenization was not enforced by Rome; she did not require the races and cities to give up their traditions, their national usages and sentiments; it was they, rather, who were eager for Greek culture and Roman citizenship.

The great German scholar, Wendland, puts it that Rome's historical task was to overcome the principle of nationality by universalism; she was to do this by linking the nations in the unity of state and eventually in the unity of church, in the unity of Roman law, which was universal, and (we may add) in the unity of that Greek culture which, after all, is the only culture our western world has ever known.

Enough for our present purpose has been said of the

Roman conquest of the world; it is our task now to look at the Roman Empire as men knew it in New Testament times, but first we must deal with the background, which haunted the minds of men. The background always does. Half the nineteenth century was haunted by the guillotine; men could not forget the Jacobins, the *émigrés*, the wars of Napoleon. In the same way, in this world of the Mediterranean the memory is indelible of the long breakdown of the republican system of Rome and the horrible disasters, in which the failure of Roman government and of Roman character involved the whole of mankind. Good and bad were so mingled in the Roman constitution that neither could overcome the other; the government could neither collapse nor recover, and the prolongation of the decline made things worse. There were, of course, there always are, people blind to what is happening. Cicero writes to Atticus about "our friend Cato" who thinks he is living in Plato's Republic (which is the Greek for More's Utopia)— and forgets that he lives "in the dregs of Romulus".[1] Cato's contribution was a stern character, a stiff mind, an insensibility to the real situation, an unflinching spirit—and a prolongation of the agony.

It is plain to anyone who thinks, though not all republicans think, that no form of government makes higher and harder demands upon its citizens than a democracy. A republic calls for the greatest possible integrity in every man, the highest and sanest political judgment, and, what is more, though less often realized, the highest possible culture to which he can

[1] Cicero, *ad Atticum*, ii, 1, 8.

aspire. All that is summed up in the most remarkable account of democracy that the world has yet seen, the speech of Pericles given in the second book of Thucydides; the demand of Athens—and it is the demand of every democracy—is that every citizen shall always aim to be better than he is, that he shall develop his own individuality, that he shall realize the world in which he lives, and that he shall dedicate himself, his powers and his knowledge, above all, his sense, his character and his ideals, to the development of the state.

To say such things may seem irony, when one looks at the story of republics, when one looks at the failure of the Roman government. Two things are wrong in Rome. The whole system of government is wrong— the extension of a constitution, suitable enough for a clan, adapted, with a minimum of change when it became a township and then a city, and kept, still with the minimum of change, to rule a vast empire; the very idea, or the absence of idea, is fundamentally wrong. In the next place, for a century and a half there is progressive moral degeneration. Plutarch tells us that when Brutus, shortly before Philippi, heard of the murder of Cicero, he blamed his friends at Rome; the fault was not in their stars, but in themselves, that they were underlings.[1] It is a pity that the enlightenment of good stupid men costs mankind so much blood.

The world always needs thought-out government, strong government; and the more complex it becomes, the more various and intricate the threads that bind it together, the greater variety of type and race, language

[1] Plutarch, *Brutus*, 28.

and tradition, that it contains, the more it demands in the government intelligence, policy, control. In all these things the men failed who held the helm; they refused to understand what the possession of the world meant; they floundered in policy, except perhaps where great campaigns with urgent need for sense were involved; they mismanaged national finance almost incredibly. Their system of taxation in the provinces it would hardly be an epigram to call brigandage, though there were laws to control it and permanent judicial commissions to deal with cases of extortion. But the plan of it was wrong; it was on a wrong basis, and not merely on a wrong basis, but worked with a wrong spirit. The sale by the state of the right to collect taxes opened the door to every kind of wickedness. The Senate had far too little control either over generals in command of armies, or over governors in charge of provinces. The whole world needed peace, but peace it did not get; one war followed another, wars provoked by ambition, unintelligent wars bungled and prolonged, and then civil war.

Meantime there was the moral decline, which prevents the development of a better form of government. It is a question whether one should blame the system for stunting the political intelligence, or blame the undeveloped intelligence for holding by an outworn system. It is the problem that conservatism everywhere offers to us; is the constitution of the United States, fortified as it is against amendment, more of a danger to Americans or to the rest of the world, a system unchanged in a century and a half of rapider development than mankind perhaps has ever seen? There is among the Roman people, first to be observed among the populace and eventually in the Senate itself, a want of training, a want of intellectual development and real education. There is again a growing impatience of discipline; and the Republic is doomed to fall as the Roman noble grows to be more and more the counterpart of Plato's democratic man:

> Myself will to my darling be
> Both law and impulse.

Plato's picture is famous of the man whose mind is a perfect democracy, whose every notion or impulse has equal rights with every other, where every fancy is on an equality with any remaining principle or ideal, in whose soul insolence and anarchy, waste and impudence, lord it in bright array, with garlands on their heads.[1] That type of man appears in Rome, and it was no miracle. There was, as we saw, no Plato to give him a new intellectual basis for a higher morality. The sense of responsibility is lost, and with it that insight into the problems of government which only the consecration of duty can produce. Ill-gotten wealth avenged itself. The political story of Rome in those last generations is one long succession of struggles for power, varied by secret murder, by general proscription, by civil war; the state cannot mend itself; every proscription promises a retaliation, and life and government grow more and more uncertain. As Livy says in his preface, "we no longer can bear our own vices nor the remedies for them".

"When a city conquers a world", says the French

[1] Plato, *Republic*, viii, 559 ff.

scholar, Grenier, "she can hardly hope to continue to be herself". Of all great movements that one may study in history, none seems so remarkable as the reaction of the Roman provinces. Conquered, crushed, powerless, with no means of making themselves felt, at the mercy of the worst rulers that chance may send them from Rome, they have a reaction, an immense reaction, on the whole of Roman history and on the Roman government. Here is a world pillaged, the eastern provinces ravaged by brigands under the Macedonian kings, ravaged in the wars which those kings waged with mercenaries, ravaged by the Roman troops and the slave-dealers who followed them, ravaged again in the civil wars of Rome, raided by the Parthian. We have a world losing population, not merely as the effect of massacres, but because men and women were losing heart and hope. It was not reserved for modern times to recognize the fact and the cause of race suicide; they are noted by Polybius. Yet the provinces change the destiny of Rome, and end the Republic; it seems like the cry of Hecuba in the play—there is justice in the world after all.[1] Somehow people felt that the world with its great past must still be capable of recovery; but where was the power that was to save it? China to-day gives us something like the spectacle of that old world; and as it seems clear that there will be no peace or order there again until there is a sovereign power that can control the whole country, so, according to Tacitus, men, looking back at the death of Augustus, agreed that there could have been no other remedy for a discordant nation

[1] Euripides, *Trojan Women*, 884–8.

than to be ruled by one man.[1] Before that man was born, everything was moving in that direction.

The provinces produced a new type of Roman, a very remarkable type. He was sent out to govern, and he learned his task by doing it. A Roman might in the course of years have experience in half a dozen provinces, in one or another magistracy, financial or military, in control, in greater or less measure, of one province after another; with the result that he developed new instincts and new capacities, and ended a very different man from what he started. The Roman magistrate, selected by a series of popular elections, which would tend at least to eliminate the less fit, and trained by experience of all sorts in many lands, replaces the descendants of Alexander's generals; and he is really better than they. Of course there were very bad cases of vicious and incompetent governors; none the less the type emerges, capable, thoughtful, and, in a curious Roman way, sympathetic with his province. From time to time, when things are at the worst, experiments are made in the concentrated rule of the single responsible man. The most famous case is the commission of the whole Mediterranean Sea, and its shores fifty miles inland, to Pompey in 66 B.C. for the abolition of piracy; and he drove the pirates off the sea in three months. The type is beginning to emerge; the experiment is being tried; and at the same time ready to the hand of the man, who realizes what has to be done and will undertake to do it, is the engine which the new army offers; and at last comes the man, Caesar.

[1] Tacitus, *Annals*, i, 9.

To understand the Hellenistic world it was necessary to linger over the personal character and mind of Alexander; and the Roman Empire, if it is to be understood, requires the same attention to the character of Caesar. When he first appears in the life of Rome, he is a young man with bright black eyes,[1] rather fastidious in the care of his person; and very soon it becomes clear that he is the cleverest, quickest and brightest of the young nobles in the party opposed to the Senate—interested in pleasure, interested in the things of the mind, possessed to the full of the great Hellenistic training, quicker in his grasp of a political situation, and shrewder as to the right step to take, than any one playing the game against him or with him. Steadily he grows in significance, as the years give him experience, and his party realizes his force of character. In 59 B.C. he is consul, and then for nine years he is away from Rome—in Gaul, as everybody knows—empire-building, if that modern phrase is permissible; for once it is true. He had the whole huge country of France to conquer, to organize, to civilize, great armies to handle, long distances to traverse in a new country without roads, great enemies to fight, and a splendid people to inspire; he did it all and made France Latin for ever. But if he shaped France, the Gauls developed him. He comes back to Rome a new man with a new grasp of facts and principles, a new realization of the world,[2] a new sense of freedom; he reshapes Rome as he had reshaped Gaul.

[1] Suetonius, *Julius*, 45.
[2] Cf. Lucan, x, 183, *mundique capacior hospes*, and the lines that follow, referring to his interest in astronomy.

Strabo[1] says that Caesar was always a lover of
Alexander, a sentence which it does one good to keep
in memory, linking the great. He has, as Mr Heitland
says,[2] a large imperial mind; he is a statesman above
all men in antiquity. No man is more essentially
Roman, but he has shared Greek culture, and he has
lived in the larger world; and, like Alexander, he
wishes to keep and to combine in a larger union everything that has been proved of value. He seems to have
thought of a world reorganized on the basis of the
monarchy that the Hellenistic kingdoms had been
developing. The central idea is a government answer-
ing to the real facts. A sentence in Suetonius' life of
him tells us how Caesar reformed the Roman calendar,
which was ninety days wrong. "He fitted the year to the
course of the sun", says Suetonius.[3] The sun, after all,
is the final authority for any calendar; and the calendar
of Julius was used for centuries, and was only superseded
in Russia about 1917. In a very similar way Caesar
fits the government of the world to the great essential
facts of the world. He is a realist, says Mommsen, and
he develops what is essentially a monarchical system—
monarchical, though not royal—where, at the head of
all, there is one brain, and a great brain, where all
others responsible for the administration have to
answer to the man, in whose hands are gathered all
the threads of government. Everything points to the
greatness of this man. To remodel the old, says Aris-

[1] C. 594.
[2] W. E. Heitland, *The Roman Republic*, §§ 1051, 1290.
[3] Suetonius, *Julius*, 40; it is memorable that Mohammed tried
to do the same thing, forbade like Julius any future intercalation,
but adjusted the calendar by the moon, with dreadful results.

totle, is as hard as to establish the new;[1] and this was Caesar's task. Roman usage was hundreds of years old, and Rome was conservative. Suetonius[2] tells us how Caesar planned, like Napoleon, to codify the law of Rome, anticipating some of the greatest of his successors. We learn too how, making a system of the government, controlling every province directly through a legate, making everybody responsible to himself, he does not plan to have it a military despotism. Great soldier as he was, he was far more than a soldier. All the time he is widening the basis of citizenship. We are told how he gave Roman citizenship to the people of Gades in the west and to the Jews of Alexandria, how he planted colonies, how he restored Corinth and Carthage which a hundred years before Rome had destroyed, and, to crown all, how he introduced into the Senate of Rome Gauls from France. It was this last act that vexed the Romans perhaps as much as anything. A ribald couplet was posted in the streets of Rome:

> Caesar led the Gauls in triumph,
> To the Senate House he led;
> And the Gauls took off their trousers,
> Put the toga on instead.

When Augustus came into control, he turned those Gauls out of the Senate, which is as significant as Julius putting them in. The great work of Caesar was the combination of good government with the spread of culture, and above all of peace on earth and goodwill among men. Those words are perhaps

---

[1] *Politics*, iv, 1, 7.　　　　[2] Suetonius, *Julius*, 44.

familiar in another connexion; but the two stories are one.

Of the civil wars that followed the murder of Caesar it is needless to speak. The world gained nothing by the silly act of Brutus. But, after a dozen years, the heir of Caesar was able to carry out his work and make it permanent. Power, says Gaston Boissier, had made Augustus a better man—a thing, he adds, not very common. We see under Augustus and his successors a new world and a new order. Augustus insists that it is restoration,[1] and, like a statesman who builds on the past, he endeavours to call up the old Roman spirit, and the poets whom he gathers about him second him. *Romanos rerum dominos gentemque togatam.* Augustus is not as great as Julius; he has more than his uncle the instincts of the Italian; but even his limitations help him at times, and he achieves a great triumph. He too, our historians tell us, had a feeling for Alexander and imitated him.[2] The greatness of his triumph is that the system which he built lasted for centuries and gave mankind immense gifts. These we have to survey. The historian Gwatkin once called the succession of the Roman Emperors the most splendid roll of names in history. Gibbon maintains that "the most happy and prosperous period in all history" (he lived of course before the Victorian Age) was from the death of Domitian to the accession of Commodus—that is to say, roughly the second century A.D. The same claim for this period was made

[1] The reader should turn to the Monumentum Ancyranum for Augustus' own recital of his aims and acts.
[2] D. G. Hogarth, *Philip and Alexander*, p. 278.

by Disraeli, in his speech proposing to make the Queen Empress of India.[1] Asquith, who was a scholar, more cautiously says that "in not a few of its aspects it has as good a title to be called the Golden Age as any era in history".[2] But one recalls the comment of J. B. Bury that this view represents rather the ideal of utilitarians than of thinkers.

But it may be better to turn to the men of the day and hear how they speak of the new government and its significance. Strabo, the contemporary of Augustus, emphasizes the great value of Roman peace—in the intercourse of nations, in the cessation of piracy, in the changed habits of Gaulish savages, in the advancement of science, notably (he adds as in private duty bound) of geography. The Roman Empire, as Alexander's had done, contributes to men's knowledge of the outer world.[3] Never before, says Strabo, had men peace so wide and so great, and such abundance of all that was good.[4] Scarcely a generation later, Philo, in the story of his legation to Rome,[5] praises Augustus in the same sense as the giver of peace and the guardian of peace. A little later comes Pliny the Elder with his magnificent phrase, *pacis Romanae immensa majestas*, "the boundless majesty of Roman peace"; and he emphasizes the great gain to life, to the intercourse of races, to knowledge of the outer world (especially including botany); and he says it is a boon given by the immortal gods to mankind.[6] So far in the first

[1] Maurois, *Disraeli*, p. 265.
[2] In his Rectorial Address at Glasgow, *Occasional Addresses*, p. 71.
[3] D. G. Hogarth, *Philip and Alexander*, p. 278.
[4] Strabo, C. 14; 144; 186; 204; 288.   [5] Philo, *Leg. ad. Gai.*, 21.
[6] Pliny, *Nat. Hist.* xiv, 2; xxvii, 3; xxxvi, 118.

century. In the second century, toward the end, we have Tertullian insisting that the Roman Empire belongs to the Christian more than to the pagan, because it was the God of the Christians who created it and put it into the hands of the Roman Emperors; the Emperor is ours, he urges, more than yours, and we pray every day for the health of the Emperor and for the permanence of the Empire—the one thing that stands between us and the end of the world; for the Empire will last to the end of the world. The same thing is said by the Syrian writer, Afrahat, in the third century. Origen[1] in the third century points out the great contribution of Roman peace, international peace, to the spread of the Christian church. In the fourth century, or at the beginning of the fifth, in passage after passage, the poet Prudentius says the same thing:[2]

Happy they! had they known that all their prosperity was God's ordaining, with Christ for their prince! For God bade the kingdoms move one after the other in a certain order. God bade the triumphs of the Roman increase, in that it was His will, when the ages should be complete, to pour Himself into them.

Whence grew that glory of thine?—Peoples discordant in speech, kingdoms diverse in culture, God willed to unite, God would submit to one rule, and God would have them in harmonious union, submitted to a gentle sway, that love of religion might hold the hearts of all mankind linked together. There is no union fit for Christ unless one mind unite all the nations together.

O Christ, the only Godhead, O splendour, O virtue of the Father, O maker of earth and sky, author of these walls of Rome, who hast set Rome's sceptre high over all things, and

[1] c. Celsum, ii, 30.
[2] Prudentius, Adv. Symm. i, 287; ii, 582 (abridged a little); Peri Stephanon, ii, 413.

ordained that the world should be ruled by the toga of Quirinus, and yield to Roman arms, that, though the nations differ, thou mightest bring their ways and usage, their tongues, their genius, their worship, into obedience to one law.

The seven authors present a remarkable unanimity in their testimony; they wrote (it is needless to say) in entire independence of one another; and their evidence deserves to be studied. Hostile criticism of the Empire is familiar in the Apocalypse of St John, where a note is struck that is heard nowhere else in the New Testament, or (I think) in the Christian Fathers.

Any opposition to the Empire that existed was in the city of Rome itself, among the dispossessed, the nobles who were no longer rulers of the world, and the men of letters who took their tone from them. Perhaps we exaggerate even their dissatisfaction under the influence of that supreme artist Tacitus. Elsewhere there was no opposition to the system. Throughout the days of the Successors the world had grown used to kings and bureaucracies, and (reserving the privilege of grumbling) did not really dislike them. How natural and normal monarchy seemed with its hierarchy of graded civil servants, is proved by the swiftness with which the same conception was adopted by the Church, even if it borrowed from the Greek city-state (and kept) the great word *ecclesia*, which belongs originally to another order of life altogether.

A little space must suffice here for an outline of the imperial system. The world's inhabitants may be grouped according to their government and their states in five main divisions.

First come Roman citizens, among whom by now are

men of most varied races and lands. St Paul, as his Latin name shows, was a Roman citizen, and in one moment of tension he tells another, who had bought his citizen rights, that he himself was born free; he is a Roman very definitely though by race a Jew born in the Greek town of Tarsus in Cilicia. Similarly there are Roman citizens in Egypt, Roman citizens in Spain and all over the world.

Next to the Roman citizens we may group the "allied" cities, chiefly survivals from earlier days, cities such as Athens and Sparta, honoured with this title for their ancient greatness. The Roman was amenable to their fame and charm, and had no wish to make subjects of them. Other cities in Asia and elsewhere, for one reason and another, received special liberties and privileges.[1]

In the third place come the provinces in two groups —the imperial provinces, where the Emperor directly ruled through legates, and the senatorial provinces, where armies were not necessary, and nobles of proconsular rank could still seem to govern as their ancestors had. The distinctions drawn by the Romans between the two sorts of province are patent in the *Acts of the Apostles*; in Cyprus and Achaea Luke distinctly calls the governor *proconsul*, as he was. Gaston Boissier in his *Roman Africa*[2] emphasizes it as remarkable that no precautions were taken against the awakening of the national spirit; Gaul once conquered is wholly conquered, he says; nor does a provincial

[1] See at large Pliny's letters to Trajan; the Emperor rather regretted, but respected, some of these treaty rights.
[2] *Roman Africa*, Engl. tr. p. 129 n.

spirit waken, in spite of the strange fact that the Roman legions were unmoved for scores of years, even for centuries together. At York, for example, the same legion is kept for generation after generation, recruited from its own sons, and yet it is centuries before there is any suggestion of the break-up of the Empire.[1] Recruiting in Italy for legionary service abroad stopped in the first century. We may note in passing Mommsen's remark to Haverfield: "Ah", he said, "you have such wonderful inscriptions in your north country; no land tells us more about the Roman army than the North of England".[2] Haverfield holds that the progress of Roman civilization in Britain was not due to the movement of a race, to immigration, but that it is perhaps the best instance·in history of the influence of a higher culture.

Fourth come the independent princes and the ruling priesthoods. Here we group such people as the various Herods and Queen Tryphaena, who, if an early legend be as true as some scholars think, may have met St Paul, and Prince Juba, a very literary prince who wrote history and was a connexion of Antony and Cleopatra. King Akbar the Dark, of Edessa, to whom (according to the story long believed among Syrians) Jesus wrote the famous letter, ruled a little kingdom just outside the Empire. With the princedoms we may group ruling priesthoods.

Last come native tribes, such as the Gauls in the mountains of Galatia, where Jerome tells us that the same speech was to be heard that was heard in

---

[1] Haverfield, *Roman Britain*, pp. 130, 169, 170.
[2] *Ib.* p. 171.

France,[1] and is still to be heard in the Highlands and Prince Edward Island.

What a pageant that world is, the immense variety, from the Atlantic to the Euphrates, of race, people and tradition, is all to be read in Strabo's fascinating book, and a great deal more than most people realize, of ancient history, of natural history and other matter. The man of science who studies plague and its transmission by the fleas of the rat, for instance, will find evidence in Strabo;[2] and to the student of the New Testament the book can be invaluable.

There are different ways of writing history, or not writing it; and it may sometimes be of value, in judging of great historical institutions, to follow the method of Robinson Crusoe on his island, and to draw up an account of the *plus* side and the *minus* side. Such a summary handling of *pro's* and *con's* must obviously involve error; things will be stated too abruptly which need modification in all sorts of ways; it will not be possible to strike a balance; but, if it is understood that the method is rough and ready, a mere matter of notes and headlines, it may serve to bring out some real features of the Roman Empire, to call attention to matters that deserve further study. With so much apology, let us for once attempt it.[3]

First of all, then, the *plus* side. Haverfield,[4] forgetting the United States, as Englishmen often do,

---

[1] Quoted by M. P. Nilsson, *Imperial Rome*, p. 184.

[2] Strabo iii, C. 165; and cf. Aristotle, *Hist. Animal.* 580 b; and Warde Fowler, *Roman Essays*, p. 167.

[3] For the benefits of the Roman Empire cf. W. E. Heitland, *Roman Republic*, § 1407; F. B. Marsh, *Founding of Roman Empire*, p. 258.

[4] Haverfield, *Study of Ancient History*, p. 28.

says that the Roman Empire was the greatest experiment that the world has yet seen in Free Trade and Home Rule. Goldwin Smith said much the same about the United States, at least so far as inter-state Free Trade is concerned. Nearly all serious students of the ancient world are at one in recognizing the vast benefits that the Empire gave; one ruler was less to be dreaded, says Freeman, than 700,000;[1] and the disappearance of the degenerate successors of Alexander's generals was no loss to mankind, Cleopatra notwithstanding. First and foremost, then, in our account, we set peace. The furious faction-fighting of the old Greek cities, of Alexandria (where the women and children took a hand in it, says Polybius), of Rome, is over for ever. No navy was needed, when the Mediterranean had become a Roman lake with no hostile forces anywhere round it; the army was reduced to the minimum required for the frontiers, for the Spanish mountains, and such places. It was a fixed principle of Augustus not to extend the Roman Empire, to allow no adventures in the forests and the jungles, but to keep peace within the borders and develop the lands Rome held.

Second, we may put the triumph of law and justice, not merely as ideals all the world over, but now as actual facts. The student of the New Testament may ask, what of Pontius Pilate, what of Felix? The answer lies in their recall and disgrace; or we may ask seriously, whether they were worse than the Herods they had replaced? But, whatever failures there were, the Emperors checked oppression by

[1] Freeman, *Essays*, vol. ii, p. 264.

governors, and insisted on a stricter justice and a
more honest finance than the world had yet seen. Of
all men the Emperor could least afford to shut his eyes
to tyranny and to pillage as the Senate had done.[1]
Good government, says Mr Heitland, is normal in the
Roman Empire.

Third, as a corollary of this, we may note the
sureness and the safety of life. A democracy is safer
where you have a predominant middle class, says
Aristotle.[2] There was freedom of trade and travel, such
as has never been since in the Mediterranean lands
and is not now. Strabo[3] tells us of the Roman roads,
and of the suppression of pirates and brigands. *Mare
pacavi a praedonibus*, is the boast of Augustus on the
monument of Ancyra. Three roads led out of London.
The reduction of time in travel is noted.[4] The great
freedom of Paul in moving about implies how the
central idea of travel as a habit is established, and it is
an index to the safety of life. What is more, a general
humanization of life is found; more and more attention was paid to the unfortunate; largesse was sent
by the Emperors to cities after earthquakes and such
disasters; and orphanages are an invention of the
Roman Empire and the Emperors. Hospitals for the
sick are a Christian addition.

Fourth, though a contradiction of this is to appear
on the other side, we may reckon the great freedom of
ideas. Local usages were observed, local cults were
allowed, schools flourished, and men were thinking,

[1] F. B. Marsh, *Founding of Roman Empire*, p. 258.
[2] *Politics*, iv, 11, 14.   [3] C. 204.
[4] See C. A. J. Skeel, *Travel in the First Century*, p. 69; a very
interesting book.

and were encouraged to think. They were not to inter-
fere with the government; but, at the same time, there
was still perhaps more freedom for the thinker in the
Roman Empire than in the United States of America
to-day—things were not so standardized and education was more various. Philosophers might be Stoic or
Epicurean, Aristotelian or Sceptic, as they pleased;
neither the government nor their neighbours resented
their freedom in speculation, or quotation, as it might
be. Polytheism is never so orthodox as the monotheistic religions; and where the tradition of culture
survives, there is always apt to be a certain freedom
unfamiliar in less developed communities. Athens will
listen to St Paul for a little.

Fifth, let us put equality, the cosmopolitan spirit.
The Empire militated against class distinctions; it was
tacitly but intelligibly opposed to a nobility; it was a
system, where automatically all citizens and non-
citizens must at last gravitate to a certain equality.
By about 212 A.D. all free men were declared citizens
and were equal. Side by side with that we have to
note the absorption into the Roman ranks of foreigners,
like the family of St Paul, and his friends Luke, Titus and
Silas, who were probably not of Italian stock. Strange
combinations of names meet us; Claudius Lysias
is a military officer in the *Acts*; Dio Cassius is a civil
servant who writes the history of Rome. Writers from
Spain are prominent in Latin literature of the first
century, and Gauls later on; Africa contributes some
very great Latin writers; and at the end, when Alaric
is at the gates, the true successor of Virgil in more ways
than one is Claudian, by birth an Egyptian Greek, in

spirit Roman, a master in Latin. Similarly the most famous Greek writer of the second century is the Syrian, Lucian of Samosata. But it is westward that Roman influence was strongest, as is shown by the spread of the Latin languages and the Roman Church.

Sixth, in close sequence, we should set the Roman Empire's steady support of Hellenism, of education and the advance of culture, all over the world. Under this heading one might put Augustus' restoration of religion, whatever it was worth; he at least emphasized the need of religion in mankind, and through the period runs an emphasis upon moral regeneration.

Last, and seventh, we have the elevation of backward races. Strabo notes that the helots of Sparta were permanently liberated by Rome.[1] But not to linger over detail, we have only to recall the wealth of Roman remains all over England south of the Wall as evidence of what for four centuries Rome did in this island, and what the Saxon invaders, the ancestors of the English, seem to have taken a pleasure in undoing. With all this we must remark Strabo's cool statement that the island was not financially worth conquering; to hold it and collect the tribute would not come to as much as customs dues on the coast of Gaul; and Appian's short sentence a century later, that the part of Britain held is not very profitable to the Romans.[2]

But now we must turn round and consider the *minus*. No golden age lasts long, says Mr Haverfield.[3] The

---

[1] Strabo C. 305–6; 365.
[2] Strabo C. 115; Appian, *Praef.* 5.
[3] Haverfield, *Roman Britain*, p. 265.

happiest period of mankind, the Victorian Age, lasted sixty-three years. "No one yet knows", writes Professor Burkitt,[1] "why the Roman Empire fell." "If you want to know why the Roman Empire fell, read Finlay", wrote John Morley.[2] Let me add another Scot's caustic comment, when he came on board ship after seeing Knossos in Crete: "The moral of Knossos is that good plumbing will not save a civilization".

First of all, it was an incalculable drawback that there was no self-determination of races in that world —they are subjects, all of them. As Appian said (A.D. 160), "in a word the Emperors were everything".[3] We may again recall how Cavour said that the worst chamber is better than the best antechamber. There lies one of the great difficulties of the Roman Empire; the Emperor's confidential freedmen managed too much in the first century,[4] and in the second (the golden age) that excellent civil service. There were no international interactions. It is good, as an Irish professor has said, for the English to have the Irish beside them; it keeps them from getting too settled in their minds. Uniformity does not afford much mental stimulus in church or state; the old dreadful era of international rivalry, with all its unrest, at least developed thought and study.

Second, there is a great deal too much government, especially after Hadrian. It was Vitellius, an unesteemed Emperor, who first founded a civil service

[1] F. C. Burkitt in *Essays Biblical*, p. 206.

[2] John Morley, *Recollections*, vol. i, p. 66.

[3] Appian, *Praef.* 6.

[4] A curious defence of these freedmen is in Sir S. Dill, *Roman Society from Nero*, p. 105.

in Rome, though Maecenas is said to have recommended Augustus to employ the knights in this way. More was done, though fitfully, by the Flavian Emperors; but it was Hadrian who fairly established the salaried civil service, with all its efficiency and all its deadly poison.[1] "There is no mood", writes Mr H. A. L. Fisher, "if it be long sustained, more dangerous to the intelligence than the imperative";[2] and that is one of the supreme reasons for the decline of the Roman Empire. The imperative is shared by the Emperor and his civil servants, for it was obviously to him alone that they were responsible. It needs a strong parliament to control public officials, and there was nothing in the Empire to protect the subjects against the servants of the rulers.

Third, the government was too good: and it is better for the development of character and contentment to do certain things badly yourself than to have them done better for you by somebody else. The great object of democracy, according to a modern humourist, who is not always so shrewd, is to keep itself from being too well governed. It is possible even for a government, as well as a church, to be "drunk with a sense of organization".

Fourth, let us put bad finance and over-taxation. We need only recall the publicans in the Gospels, their oppressiveness and the hatred they earned so well. The tax-collectors and the administrators cost the human spirit more and more as time went on, crushing

[1] See B. W. Henderson, *Emperor Hadrian*, pp. 64–67; Dill, *loc. cit.* p. 107.
[2] *Napoleon*, p. 191.

energy and enterprise; and what they gave was not worth to mankind what it cost. We have, of course, not to forget the wasteful purchase of luxuries from the East, at a cost of a million sterling a year, Pliny says, in precious metals, as a factor in financial breakdown; there was very little that the Orient cared to buy from the Mediterranean world—red coral, but little else; and gold and silver drained back to Arabia and India.

In the next place, whether this is economic or spiritual, slavery vitiates life. It was not peculiar to Rome; but it meant, as Mr Heitland[1] emphasizes, that there was not in the fields "that loving care which agriculture needs"; there was no improvement in tool or method. All round there is a deadening of invention and a shirking of work. The masses are poor; the farmers begin to be turned into serfs; the cultivator belongs to the land, and not the land to the farmer. Further, in spite of slave fidelity and the frequent friendship between owner and slave (as between Cicero and his Tiro), there is the boundless spiritual loss that slavery always means, the contempt for marriage implied by the mating of slaves, by the concubinage of master and slaves, the degradation of character which the freedom to inflict cruelty on slaves always induces. The gladiatorial shows were, in a sense, the outcome of slavery; it was abuse of the captive. The reaction of all these things on the spirit, on the mind, on the conscience and on the soul of mankind, is beyond calculation.

Sixth, comes standardization. Everything is made

[1] Heitland, *Agricola*, p. 159.

too uniform, the discipline is too efficient, the training makes people too like one another. It is probable that to-day, both in America and in England, the efficiency of education, with the dominance of government officials in education, is effecting a similar standardization which must lead in the long run to a decline of intelligence and culture; admirable and progressive as our sturdy enforcement of system seems at present, it is too like the efficiency of Hadrian's knights, a step forward with unseen dangers involved. Longinus discusses whether democracy was not after all the nursing-mother of genius, whether literature rises and falls with democracy; to-day, he says, we learn from infancy the lessons of a righteous slavery and are swathed in its customs and observances, and find slavery the cage of the soul cramping all growth.[1] The persecution of the Christian church, and the utilization of such persons as Ignatius of Antioch for the arena, follow from this insistence on government control of religion, from the government's resentment of any independent organization. For till the authorities realized the existence of a church, they cared nothing about Christian propaganda.

With the decline of intelligence comes the decline of spirit. The great evil of despotism, it has been said, is the gradual destruction of thought. Freeman emphasizes the same thing, the crushing of nearly all intellectual life.[2] Martha speaks of the general discouragement.[3] There is no real opening for ambition.

Cromwell, I charge thee, fling away ambition—

[1] Longinus 44.   [2] Freeman, *Essays*, ii, 335.
[3] Martha, *Les Moralistes*, p. 210.

it may be a very suitable thing for a fallen cardinal to say, but it will not do; it is a fatal rule for a community; ambition and competition may be sins for a churchman, but for the mass of men they are more like virtues; the well-being of the state depends on them.

There was no opening for real ambition for young men, in the Empire, except as civil servants or soldiers; and there was little chance to become a soldier and to rise in the army unless a man were a barbarian from over the border or born in the army. The Roman power of assimilation, however, flags, we are told by Mr Heitland, after A.D. 100.

Eighth, comes gradual depopulation and gradual impoverishment. It began in Greece, when Alexander planted his seventy cities in the East, and his successors followed his example, and the Greeks emigrated to the new places. But many things made for it. Asia Minor perhaps never quite recovered from Sulla's treatment. Plague, taxation, and loss of spirit, bring down the birth-rate.[1]

Last and ninth, summing it all up, it is all too like Plato's horrible *Republic*; a term is set to all progress. The Roman Empire in its worst days is the mother of the Roman Catholic church, stereotyped in contrast with that ceaseless spirit of progress which is the genius of real Christianity and which the Christian church owes above all to her Master. It needed the barbarian invader, the Renaissance and the Reformation to free the human spirit.

[1] See George Finlay, *Greece under the Romans*, ch. i, § 7.

VII

THE HELLENISTIC TOWN

It is a commonplace that to generalize is to be wrong, at least in some degree; but without generalization it is sometimes difficult to convey ideas at all. With this caution it may be possible to attempt some picture of the ancient town, as men saw towns in the Roman Empire, particularly the Hellenistic town, with a glance perhaps at times at the Roman town of the West. The city of Rome itself must be excluded; it is chiefly the eastern Mediterranean that concerns us. What has to be said falls easily into three parts.

First, we have to consider the external aspects of the town or city; and then to turn our attention to the life in its streets, the movements and pre-occupations that capture attention from the outward structures; and, in the third place, it may help us to take the greatest city of them all, and, in studying what we may call its contribution to the life and thought of mankind, to see something of what was intended by the founders of the great Hellenistic cities, and by the great soldier and administrator who gave them the idea that such cities were to be a real factor in the life of mankind.

First, then, the city and its outward aspect. Any ancient town in our modern world—Cambridge or London will be all the examples needed—will tell you by the mere shape of its streets, their irregularity in breadth and direction, how from some primitive village, with a very minimum of foresight, the town has struggled into being, which, in some cases, becomes the nucleus of a great city. The features of it are familiar. In Cambridge St John's Street and the short streets prolonging it, were once all of them one street with one name, High Ward. Its history is written in its shape for those who can master a palimpsest. The Hospital of St John and the lane by its side that led down to the river are gone; the Jewry and All Saints' Church are gone; but the street winds its narrow way as of old to where southward it lies open in King's Parade, broad and magnificent,[1] and thence past the site of the ancient Trumpington gate into the open road to London. But we have to remember that between the University Library and the University Church there were once streets and rows of houses; the great lawn of King's College by the river replaces a mass of houses, streets and wharves; the broken ends of the Mill Street it cut in two still lie in front of Trinity Hall and Queens' College. The twisted street, the narrow lane, all over England and France, bear witness to the old town which grew, which never had a founder, and which, you might almost say, never had even a Town Council endowed with any kind of foresight. There is a charm about some of these old towns, an individuality, something unmistakable, almost personal, which the more modern towns fail as yet to develop. Bryce remarked forty years ago on the uniformity of the newer American towns, especially westward, and the author of *Main Street*, if in nothing

[1] These adjectives are to be taken as relative to Cambridge or Bristol rather than Winnipeg.

beyond his title, hints at their monotony from Alleghanies to Rockies. The Hellenistic towns were like them in being new and laid out to a plan; and in both cases one concludes that it has been a standard plan.

No one, I think, would wish to remodel London to be a counterpart of modern New York; but no one, who is not a romantic of an extreme type, would ever dream of planning a new city quite on the lines of London or of old New York; it would more probably be on the lines of Winnipeg with its broad thoroughfares and right angles. Town planning in the western and modern world seems hardly older than Philadelphia; in the ancient world it goes back to Archidamus of Miletus, who suggested it for the Piraeus. It is very curious to find in Aristotle's *Politics* an anticipation of Napoleon III and Baron Haussmann, who did away with the old narrow and winding streets of Paris and laid out broad streets that were straight. The Baron and the philosopher had the same idea. Aristotle[1] notes the superior value of the crooked lanes for street fighting. Nowadays in an age of developed athletics street fighting is of less importance: in the Middle Ages it was perhaps the only available form of effective athletics in Cambridge and many another disorderly university town. But the founders of the great cities of the Hellenistic world, which becomes the Roman world, had no more mind than Napoleon for faction fights, barricades and insurrections, and their accommodation. Certain great features of their towns are to be noted. The street was to be broader than the primitive town knew, nothing like broad

[1] *Politics*, iv, 11, p. 1330.

enough for us to-day as you feel, if you visit what is left of them.[1] Neither the ancients, nor the moderns, except by accident, ever dreamt of motor traffic. But the city should be foursquare, with rectangular blocks of buildings, all the streets if possible crossing at right angles. It is the simplest plan for convenient traffic; and it was so generally accepted, so pleasant to the ancient mind, that, when in the Apocalypse the Holy City descends from Heaven, it proves to be laid out on very much the same plan. Whatever our conception of the picturesque, the heavenly Jerusalem, with all its splendours of gold and precious stones, could not be thought of with the ground plan of some of our queer old towns; it is rectangular and so far, to English ideas, a trifle dull. But it reveals the mind of the ancients.[2]

But the founders of the new Hellenistic cities also meant that they should be cities indeed and not mere country boroughs. They planned a town of peace, a town of commerce and a town of beauty. It is very interesting to find a book, ante-dating Alexandria by half a century, and attributed to Xenophon, which deals with Athens herself, almost as a highly en-lightened and progressive modern would deal with some old English town, if he were trying to induce the mayor and corporation to take in new ideas as to the town's future. The writer puts before his fellow-citizens the great fact that Athens is haunted by two types of visitor, by the commercial man—shipping people and

[1] The pictures of Pompeii are familiar. The reader should visit Rhodes, if he can, to see a wonderful medieval town with memorable streets.

[2] See generally Haverfield, *Ancient Town Planning*, especially pp. 41, 55; and *Roman Occupation of Britain*, pp. 214 ff.

traders—for whom the Piraeus is of supreme importance as a centre of distribution: but the city is also
visited by people who are thinking of things of the
mind, by people who want to see its beauty. Amongst
other things he positively recommends the building of
what we should call first-class hotels. Probably any
such hotels as he had in mind, or were actually built,
we should not call first-class at all, nor our great-
grandfathers either. But he has the conception of the
city beautiful and the city thoughtful, planned and
practicable, but not greatly remodelled. For Athens,
as her citizens well knew, was the most beautiful city
in the world.

Athens set a standard of beauty to all builders of
cities. Plutarch, writing rather later than St Paul,
speaks of that Parthenon, under the shadow of which
Paul preached on Mars Hill, as being still in its
marvellous beauty as fresh as if the sculptors had just
left it; and it was five hundred years old. So old was
the idea of adorning your city with splendid buildings.
The idea was not lost; it was quickly caught up by the
great city builders, and developed. In the ancient
Greek world a splendid building stood by itself; and,
except where nature provided an Acropolis to tower
above the city, it might be uncomfortably and in-
artistically jammed in among houses, and shops, and
all sorts of things, which would ruin the general effect
from an aesthetic point of view. But, from the days of
Alexandria onward, the town and its buildings are
more definitely planned with a view to their total
effect, to a general aspect, which, taken as a thought-
out whole, should impress the visitor; the great

building, which is to be the envy of all other towns, is to stand in a setting that will allow its splendour to be realized, and the aesthetic value of open spaces is recognized. All over the world we find evidence of this passion for the well-planned city, with the rectangular streets, the great buildings and the impressive setting.[1] Dr J. S. Reid in his book on the municipalities of the Roman Empire remarks that the Roman world could show quite insignificant towns with buildings to match a modern capital. Anyone who has travelled even a little in Provence will remember the amazing amphitheatres, at Nîmes and Arles, towns strangely near one another; and these are not the only ones. The feeling that a real city should have an amphitheatre, must have come from Rome, and it shows how fashions in splendour spread. A modern parallel would be the imperative need which every rising university in America feels to have a stadium larger than the Yale "Bowl"—an amphitheatre in fact built to seat more than three times as many spectators as that at Nîmes, but, if intended for a less cruel sport, of necessity essentially like it in design.[2]

The Greek city is adorned more often with porticoes, basilicas, public baths, an aqueduct, a theatre and temples. In Pliny's letters to Trajan, written about A.D. 110 from Bithynia, we read of ambitious building schemes taken up by this town and that town, some-

[1] See Rostovtzeff, *Anc. Hist.* vol. I, *Orient and Greece*, p. 391.

[2] On Nîmes see for instance David Macgibbon, *Architecture of Provence and the Riviera*, p. 66. He says the Nimes Arène seats 20,000, and is smaller than that of Arles. The Yale Bowl seats 75,000, and is full whenever the Yale–Harvard football match is played.

times with most disastrous results alike in finance and construction. The theatre, the splendid theatre, of Nicaea (which cost half a million dollars), has insecure foundations, it cracks badly, and is dangerous. The aqueducts of Nicomedeia were to be magnificent, but they failed to bring water to the city. Pliny writes anxiously to the Emperor begging for Roman architects; and the Emperor more than once tells him that he can get Greek architects. Pliny writes that he knows he can get Greek architects, but he does not want them, for reasons which can be surmised.[1] Some things that to-day we should consider necessary to a city, more necessary perhaps than colonnades, were not thought so important. The lighting of streets was not much thought of westward, but someone in our period speaks of the illumination of Alexandria by night as "the sun in small change".[2] The phrase will appeal to anyone who has looked by night at New York, from the Eagle Rock at Montclair. The disposal of sewage in Rome impressed Strabo, as we saw; but it never could be with Greeks so much a passion and a religion as with some of our reformers.[3] But beauty meant more to them, and for the Hellenistic king beauty was translated into splendour.

It was a favourite form of public generosity, in the Hellenistic lands, for centuries, to give one's city some

---

[1] Pliny, *Epp.* x, 37–40; Macgibbon, *loc. cit.* p. 66, comments on "vicious construction" at Nîmes; yet it has lasted.

[2] Quoted by Mahaffy, *Empire of Ptolemies*, p. 97, from Achilles Tatius, ἥλιος κατακερματίζων.

[3] Pliny, *Epp.* x, 98, Amastris, alongside its very beautiful and very long street, has a very disgusting and very smelly open sewer, which they *call* a river.

great building, baths perhaps or a gymnasium or a colonnade. *Gymnasiis indulgent Graeculi,* writes Trajan.[1] One of the most interesting is at a town very little known to-day, perhaps never well known—Oinoanda. There one Diogenes, otherwise entirely unknown, combining public generosity and missionary ardour, erected a colonnade, and a fine one, the walls of which he inscribed with the teaching, maxims and letters of Epicurus. The colonnade added, we must suppose, something of beauty to his city; it was a boon, a public benefit, a shelter against sun and rain; and it pointed its fellow-citizens the way to the ideal life—free from anxiety and free from the fear of death. Another man would build and endow a public library. But the greatest of all the builders was Herodes Atticus in the first quarter of the second century A.D. His father, according to the story, had found an immense hidden treasure, too big to be kept with safety. He offered it to the Emperor of the day as a measure of safety, but he was told to keep it and use it. What he did with it seems not known, but his son's gifts were of the most profuse to Athens, and to many other towns besides Athens. To this day it is familiar how a Greek will do the same thing. The modern stadium at Athens, erected within the last few years by a rich Greek from the new world, is a close parallel. To the university, as we should call it, that might be in the city, we must return at a later point. But before we leave the story of royal and private generosity shown in decorating the cities with permanent structures of beauty, some word must be spared for the amazing and incredible

[1] Pliny, *Epp.* x, 40.

traditions in some of the Hellenistic cities of pageants of perfectly inconceivable luxury and waste. Several descriptions of them survive, notably from Alexandria and Antioch, where wealth and gold and silver and works of art and clothing and all sorts of things were paraded. What useful purpose it served except to keep the people in a good temper and to impress them with the riches and the implied power of the king, we may well ask.

Dr J. S. Reid has suggested that "the flourishing state of thousands of civic communities all over the Empire refutes the tales of general agricultural decay". But it is surely arguable that all this profuse building may have contributed to the decay of the Roman world; for the cost of construction must have been enormous, and the bigger the buildings the larger the cost of upkeep. Impressive as the Nîmes amphitheatre is, few ancient remains speak so forcibly to the visitor from the North; it is a monument of wastefulness and speaks of cruelty.

The government of the Hellenistic city was modelled in the main on that of the self-governing Greek town, but it was always subject to a rescript from the Macedonian king, the successor of Alexander, and, later on, to the interference of the Romans, of the neighbouring proconsul or of the Emperor, as we can see in the letters of Pliny. The interference may have been warranted, or not, in any particular case, but it limited freedom. There is a good deal of evidence that local government became more and more paralysed as the Roman Empire grew older, perhaps as a result of Greek decline, perhaps also of the aggressive development of the civil service. In one point, as we have noticed, there is a distinct advance. The modern historian of the Hellenistic world,[1] as we saw, says they had real lawyers at last, and real courts of justice supported by royal and later by imperial authority, instead of popular assemblies like the Heliaea of Athens—where, as a well-known Oxford scholar has said with only too much truth, "all their trials were parodies". The development is one outcome of Alexander's work. The codes of law of the various places naturally differ; if there is a tendency to model them on Athens, the local code has to vary with the region and with the traditions of the more numerous race. In Syria, for instance, there is a Syrian element in the law, if the tone of society is none the less Greek.

In passing to the second part of our subject, the social life in the town, perhaps it is as well to begin with the streets. One of the most caustic pages of Polybius is that in which he describes the mongrel race of Alexandria, matched by another page in an earlier part of his work where he describes the horrible riots which disgraced the city in the second century—riots, a political term for a political purpose—furious attacks on the palace ending in the public murder of the unpopular minister, and the dragging of his family naked, on their backs, through the streets; and "in this", he says, "the women and the little children take their part".[2] That is how a Greek of the old Greece

---

[1] See W. W. Tarn, *Hellenistic Civilization*, pp. 77, 78, 127.

[2] Polybius xv, 27–30 (the riots); xxxiv, 10 (the mongrel race); xxii, 17 (the brutal king). Cf. E. R. Bevan, *Ptolemaic Dynasty*, pp. 100–1, on Polybius' feeling.

and the old tradition thinks of Alexandria and its ways. Two hundred and fifty years later the genial and gracious Dio Chrysostom admonishes the Alexandrians on their evil ways, as to which the Jews could have contributed their testimony before Dio and after him.

"Your city", says Dio to the Alexandrians,[1] "is remarkable in size and situation; it stands out as second city in the world. Your city is the head of which Egypt is the body, or rather Egypt is the mere appendage. To such praise you are accustomed; it is what you expect. Yet it is not you that I have praised; to dwell upon the excellence of your water is but to praise your wells; the praise of men is orderliness, gentleness, concord, good government, resistance to the temptations of pleasure. What report do strangers take away from your city? We have seen a city, they say, wonderful, glorious, but a city driven mad by song and horse-racing, a city engaged in nothing worthy of its greatness. As soon as her citizens set foot in stadium or theatre, they are bewitched; after a devastating conflagration of excitement, the turmoil and disorder smoulder on for days, consuming whatever relics have escaped the general blaze. None of you ever handled a horse; you are like lame men quarrelling over a race. Music is your curse: you are quick enough to condemn a discord in the theatre; discord among yourselves passes unnoticed. Your theatre rings with applause and uproar. For righteousness you care nothing; hence your strife, your unavailing disappointments, your senseless triumphs. Of

[1] See Barrow, *Slavery in the Roman Empire*, p. 219; I borrow the translation.

genuine civic patriotism you know nothing; empty
honours and rewards are expected by your rulers;
those who speak in your assemblies have no thought for
the common interest; they seek merely to parade themselves. To go to Alexandria is like going to see a beautiful
house, and finding its master a good-for-nothing
slave, not even fit to open the door to the visitor."

But not every Hellenistic city was so disorderly as
Alexandria and Antioch. All over the Greek world
there was still a great enthusiasm for athletics. In
every Greek city the palaestra, the wrestling-ground, is
a feature. We have seen[1] the indignation of the old-
style Jew, as he tells of the young priests hurrying down
from the Temple, stripping naked, wrestling like
Greeks, and, as a last touch of degradation, donning
the Greek hat. We read in Plutarch of the palaestra,
the wrestling-ground, at Tarsus in Cilicia: it comes in
by accident—the young men are busy with their
athletics when the wonderful ship comes up the river
Cydnos, and they leave their sports to see Cleopatra
disposed as Aphrodite amid her Nymphs and Cupids
in that famous scene, which Shakespeare describes in
Antony and Cleopatra.[2] Two hundred years separate
Maccabees and the collected Pauline Epistles, and one
wonders how far Jewish opinion had really moved.
Was the young son of Pharisees at Tarsus allowed to go
and see the heathen wrestling and running naked in
the Greek way? If that question is difficult to answer,
another question is much easier: Did St Paul as a boy
go and see the sports? His metaphors answer the

[1] Chapter v, p. 94.
[2] Plutarch, *Antony*, 25; *Antony and Cleopatra*, Act ii, scene 2.

question; "run to win!" he cries. It seems obvious that, like an ordinary boy, he watched such things, and himself raced and boxed with his school-fellows, permitted or unpermitted.

There is a great multiplication of games all over the world. Antioch on the Orontes had at one time great athletic contests. Olympia has lost its ancient significance as a centre of life, though athletes still came there from all over the world. With the widening of the kingdoms, with the coming of the Roman Empire, with the advent of a reign of peace, brought by the great powers, there was less need for that truce of God, which the Olympic festival had been. There was little of the ennobling left in Greek athletics; they occupied people's minds; but they had little real influence; a Pindar in these times was unthinkable. The professional athlete is still a popular figure, and a proverb for vanity. Even women took part in the competitions, as in these days in golf and tennis. In some places chariot-racing was the popular amusement; and westward there was the gladiatorial show: to the credit of the Greek world it was never so popular there as in the West.[1]

All through the eastern world the cities abound in *eranoi*, friendly societies, guilds and burial clubs and dining clubs. They have all sorts of names[2]—*orgeones*—people who celebrate special rituals: *thiasotai*—a more

---

[1] On the games see Mommsen, *Provinces*, i, 287-9; and E. N. Gardiner's interesting *Olympia* and his *Greek Athletic Sports and Festivals*.

[2] See T. Wilson, *St Paul and Paganism*, ch. v, pp. 121-6. Cf. J. S. Reid, *Municipalities*, pp. 513-8, for such clubs, guilds or groups westward; *seribibi* (we won't go home till morning); *furunculi* (a very honest name, or half-honest, as a man once professed himself to me); the *schola* (a place of meeting); etc.

or less religious term: *eranistai*—a club where everyone contributes his subscription. We have on some stone a record of a club of *hymnodoi*—people who sang hymns, one supposes, in honour of the local god or goddess, or the divinity of the place of their own origin. Other terms were *speira*, *taxis*, *phyle*; *synergion* concerned trades, and meant very possibly something like a trade union, except that strikes were few in that age. There is also the more familiar word *agape*, the group's meal. It is clear that these friendly societies existed for all sorts of purposes. There is, for instance, a guild of theatrical artists on record. The society may sometimes be a national re-union of immigrants, like a Greek or an Italian club in a modern American city. In these cities of the ancient world the friendly society would often consist of people from the same quarter of the Mediterranean, and an essential part of the club business would be the worship of the national god or goddess of the region from which they came; so that the friendly society is in a sense a door through which the foreign cult may spread into a new city. We have already noticed[1] the synagogue as primarily a place of worship as it is to-day; but with the usual organization of the Jews before us, and the parallel of the other national groups, it seems to assume a larger sphere of life than it might to-day in Manchester or New York. The *Acts of the Apostles* is evidence enough of the use made of it for spreading a new religion. But this brings us to think again of the burial club. There is some evidence to show that the first legal, or semi-legal, position accorded to the Christian Church was that of

[1] Chapter v, pp. 103–106.

a burial club. At any rate at the end of the second
century A.D., Tertullian tells us that one of the regular
war-cries of the mob, when they were thirsty for
Christian blood, was not always *Christianos ad leones*
but it was constantly *Ne sint areae*—"No more of their
graveyards". The spiritual fervour of the old religion
would find its outcome in harrying the dead Christian
from his grave, in whole or in part, says the apologist.
In the West we find the same sort of group, *collegia* as
they are called there. It is interesting that our familiar
word "college" means originally a society, as in some
favoured places it still does. We also meet educational
charities for the upbringing of orphans. These, however, were often imperial in their origin.

All through the cities, of course, we find the shops,
not merely in the sense of places where articles are
displayed for sale, but also where they are made. The
reader of the New Testament remembers the silver-
smith, the tent-maker, the builder and carpenter. St
Luke does not say it, and hardly needs to say it, but
analogy from the modern Levant suggests that it is
natural to picture Demetrius and his fellow-workmen
as having their shops all together in the same street.
The street of potters, the street of butchers, are familiar
sights. A great deal of the work of manufacture in the
craftsmen's places was done by slaves, as large part of
the domestic work was done, and some of the slaves
were mechanics of a high grade, even artists. We are
constantly reminded that, after the great era of pillage
by governors was over, when to the indignation of the
Greek city the Roman took away the old works of art,
mass-production of works of art, especially statues,

was a leading industry in the Hellenistic world. "Roman copies" were required and made in quantity; and, whatever their quality, we at least have no ground for regretting that the work of the great artists was constantly reproduced. The wall-paintings of Pompeii, some thousands in number, represent another art, not perhaps very original, but illustrative of the taste of the age; they are very largely mythological in subject. The manufacture of artistic *stelai*, or memorials, still went on. The reader of Lucian will recall how he hated the hereditary sculpture business. The slaves, East and West, would be of very mixed origin, as we can see in the surviving inscriptions of old Athens, and, as appears in various ways, in Rome.

Athens had long had her population of foreigners, including Asiatics from Asia Minor, and from Syria, as the cult of Adonis proves in the fifth century B.C. With all this influx of Orientals westward, with the planting of Greek cities eastward, it is easy to imagine that there was progressively a great deal of intermarriage among the races. There is some evidence that for a while Greek settlers in Egypt fetched wives from Greece.[1] But among the lower orders, where women cannot be locked up, and where there is that absence of religious barriers which seems to go with polytheism everywhere but in India, pride of race was little safeguard. We can trace it in the names: amazing and incredible oriental names are found in Greek families. Parents in classical Greece had not the Englishwoman's romantic habit of giving children indiscriminately Highland, Hebrew or Welsh

[1] Cf. the marriage contracts in G. Milligan, *Greek Papyri*.

first names whatever the surname; the strange foreign names were given by them to put the children, as in modern Hinduism, under the protection of a god or goddess. It is interesting to note in our period the growing frequency of names which imply the relation between the child and the particular god or goddess, "theophoric" names. They had been in use from very early days; the parents of Herodotus called him "Gift of Hera" and his brother "Gift of God"; perhaps they were twins. Now the names ending in -*dotus* and -*dorus* seem more frequent. It reveals the intermixture of races and of religions, for which there is abundant evidence elsewhere.

No account of the Hellenistic world would be adequate, which passed over the university centres, as we should now call them.[1] The two most famous are Athens and Alexandria. Universities were not organized in the terribly efficient and administrative way, to which, alas! we have come here in our modern zest for the "mass-production" of culture. There were not even the medieval colleges, which still, in spite of all so-called reforms, are more potent in Oxford and Cambridge than the university with its faculties, laboratories and diplomas. There was not in Athens or Alexandria our mania for examinations; the Ph.D. degree was not given. But teachers and pupils are found in groups, groups with a strong corporate spirit, as a well-known story shows. The young freshman (νέηλυς) arrives in Athens proposing to attend the lectures of a certain professor, or, more strictly, orator or philosopher. Wandering in the streets on his first

[1] See John W. H. Walden, *Universities of Ancient Greece.*

evening, he is captured by a "chorus", a band, as we should call them in English phrase, of undergraduates. "Students" is the medieval and the American term; in Athens they had all sorts of names—learners, listeners, *stasiotai*, *pôloi* and *thremmata* (colts and babes). He is captured by the band and kept in durance until he undertakes not to go to the lectures of the "sophist", whose name perhaps had actually brought him to Athens, but to join the "chorus" of his captors and "listen" to their man.[1] A certain amount of academic disorder seems appropriate; as the poets say

> The due vicissitudes of rest and toil
> Make labour easy and renew the soil.

From one source and another we can see how much what we might call the university meant to the town of Athens, with its Academy where Plato taught, the painted Porch where Zeno gave his discourses, and "the little house of Socrates". Through these first two centuries, such people as Aulus Gellius cherish fragments of the lectures they heard, and sometimes publish their notebooks. Gellius affectionately called his collection of notebooks *Attic Nights*. That horror of education is happily extinct. Tarsus had its school, which was a Stoic school, and to it went large numbers of the youth of the city. They also went abroad to study at the other centres of learning, but they did not come back: like the Scottish universities, Tarsus trained more good men than it could keep. So we learn from Strabo.

[1] This at least is true for the fourth century A.D.; see Walden, *loc. cit.* ch. 14.

As to the moral tone of the Hellenistic town, it is very difficult to know how to discover or assess the moral tone even of a modern town; it must be harder still when the evidence is two thousand years old. We are, of course, warned not to trust "the polemical superlatives of the fathers of the Church"; but the worst things about that world are told by Juvenal. But, when a man deliberately sets out to write satire, he practically tells you not to take him too seriously. Deissmann emphasizes the immense amount of evidence on moral conditions which the papyri from Egypt have given us in late years.[1] References enough to vice and crime, he says, constant evidence of more or less organized prostitution, for example; but brighter colours too, and the common people "stand before us laughing and scolding, loving and mean, malicious and kindly". Perhaps among the most illuminative are three documents, which we may take as typical[2]—the jolly letter in dreadful spelling from the boy Theon, written to his father telling him that if he will not take him with him to Alexandria, "I won't write you a letter, or speak to you, or say Good morning to you"; the contract made by the village council of Bacchias in the Fayûm for the hire of two dancing girls to perform in the village at some approaching festival for ten days, at 36 drachmas per day, a certain measure of wheat, fifteen couple of delicacies, and the use of three asses for their journey out and back; and so much earnest

[1] Adolf Deissmann, *Paul*, pp. 43–6.

[2] G. Milligan, *Greek Papyri*, Nos. 42; 45; 12. To estimate the value of the performances ($\lambda\epsilon\iota\tau\text{o}\upsilon\rho\gamma\epsilon\hat{\iota}\nu$) it should be recalled that the labourers in the vineyard had one Roman penny = one drachma per day.

in advance; and the date is added, the 3rd year of the Emperor with twelve names given in full (A.D. 237); and the letter of the man Hilarion who writes to his wife, Alis, hoping she is not worrying, and "as soon as we receive wages, I will send them to you", and asking whether she had been confined, and "if it is a boy, let him live; if it is a girl, put it out". He directs the virtual murder of the little girl in passing, as one might say, as if it were the natural thing that anybody would do with a girl baby. It is such "natural", unstudied utterances that reveal moral outlooks. If Paul is liberal, as some critic puts it, with his gloomy colours in the first chapter of his letter to the Romans, no serious student of the classics is at a loss for abundant evidence that Paul is simply stating what everybody knew. Plenty of other people point to a dark morality here and there in the great cities. Polybius remarks, for example, that Alexandria was studded with statues of Kleino carrying a little jug and wearing only a χιτών (a chemise). Kleino was a mistress of Ptolemy II, and he had the city decorated with statues of her in this garb or lack of garb. It is perhaps symbolic; even Nell Gwyn is not so depicted to please Charles II. But the matter may be put more fairly thus; let us suppose we know the worst of our great cities, such as London, Chicago or New York; will a pagan city be worse or better? Anyone with personal knowledge of great heathen cities of the East will not expect too much of the ancient city. In the English and the American city, even in their worst areas, religion is working for morality; in the Greek pagan city, and in the Roman city, it was not working for morality; in

Corinth it was working against morality. Corinth was famous for its temple of Aphrodite with some hundreds of sacred prostitutes, a temple of the type still found in India, wherever Hinduism flourishes uncontrolled and uncriticized. Little wonder that St Paul implores Christian women among the Corinthians to be ultra-conservative in dress and manners—as, we learn elsewhere, the women were at Tarsus, his own home.

Alexander founded some seventy cities, we are told, the most famous of them the Egyptian Alexandria. Well planned as to site, safe from silt which the Nile brought down, safe from the west wind which made some harbours impossible in that area, and supplied by nature with fresh water, it had many advantages. Otherwise the site was as dull as Cambridge, flat and sandy as Chicago. But it became a magnificent city and the pattern of many more.

In what is left of this chapter it remains, by study of what Alexandria was in its higher aspects, of the influence it exerted and the great contributions it made to mankind, to try to form some idea of what was in the mind of its founder. That he foresaw all that followed, it would be foolish to assert, yet Alexandria fulfilled the genius of its creator. Above all other cities of the East, above all other cities of the world except Rome, Alexandria was a meeting-ground of the races, for the Jew, the Greek, the Indian, the Arab, the Roman. It was a very great city, with huge buildings and great blocks of them; the Canopic street, we are told, was four miles long. It was the centre of a very widespread trade, the centre through which half the westward trade of India passed. It is not always remembered that from the days of Christ (which allows us a margin of twenty or thirty years) the Greek merchants of Egypt knew and used the monsoon. They called it *Hippalos*, after the Greek sailor Hippalos who first discovered its nature and made use of it. In the middle of the first century we are told that every year dozens of ships would sail for India and return. Masses of Roman coinage are found from time to time in southern India; and all the trade, implied by shipping and coinage, after reaching Egypt, passed through Alexandria. The immense wheat production of Egypt fed Rome; it was in a wheat ship of Alexandria that Paul sailed for Rome and was wrecked.

Such is the city whose life and people exercised a profound influence alike on Greek thought and the thought of the world. Early in its story the famous Museum was founded; and there, in the enormous library, with its hundreds of thousands of manuscripts, learning flourished more than anywhere else in the world—learning and natural science. Eratosthenes, the great geographer, may represent the science; Aristarchus, the great critic of Homer, and Callimachus, the prince of Alexandrine literature, may stand for the learning, while Apollonius "of Rhodes", as he chose to be called when he quarrelled with the Alexandrians, for learning and a higher achievement in poetry than the rest of the school. He at least has this distinction that Virgil admired him and drew ideas from him. It is not quite the case of Milton and Du Bartas, for Apollonius can still be read with interest and admiration. But, in general, the learning overshadowed the literature, and the school produced chiefly what a German scholar has called "professor-poetry"; it has in it too much of the lexicon and not enough of the "madness" noted by Plato. A contemporary Greek from somewhere else has a charming picture of the professors singing "in the birdcage of the Muses" at Alexandria. Alexandria contributed to Greek art, especially in the direction of realism and ornament, and, in particular, such types, we are told, as the crouching Aphrodite. Through its great writers Alexandria influenced profoundly the literature of Rome and our own literature. Theocritus scarcely belonged to the Museum, but at one time he too haunted Alexandria; in one of his poems he gives us the most pleasing picture we have of its people; and his idylls inspired in turn Virgil, Spenser and Tennyson, a great contribution to literature. To return to the science, especially the geography, it is illuminative to remember that large part of the impulse toward the discovery of America came from a regained knowledge of the geographers of Alexandria, based on their belief in a spherical globe. Nor must we forget Euclid and the centuries for which he taught Europe, as he might yet to our own great gain.

In the next place Alexandria had a great influence on the development of Greek religion. Serapis is the outstanding figure; he is a curiously composite god and is therefore typical of our period and prophetic of the great movement toward syncretism in religion, the massing and blending and philosophizing of all cults, which was the last great challenge of the ancient world to Christ. Ptolemy II is said to have fetched him from somewhere on the Black Sea. Whatever the god was originally, his migration gave him, or allowed him to develop, Egyptian features, and his new name (whether he had one before or not) shows that he combines Osiris and Apis. If all this is true, he is a rare example of an artificial god, but perhaps we are relying too much on Greek story. Late Greek theory as to the origins of gods must strike the modern student of religion as highly naïve; its suggestions are so innocent of knowledge as to the actual way in which cults develop. It was in the temples of Serapis, particularly in the greatest of all, the Serapeum, that there developed a monastic system, which, it is easy to see, influenced, if it not altogether inspired, the first Christian monks; they were Egyptians, and historically it was from Egypt that the monastic ideal spread to the West. The story of Egyptian monachism has much in it that is pitiful and degrading, far remote from the mind of Christ; yet it should be remembered how the story of Antony affected Augustine at the crucial moment of his life. Thus, while we see the spread of Egyptian ideas, Egyptian gods (especially Isis and Serapis) and Egyptian rites from Alexandria all over the Greek world, bringing new ideas of ritual and new conceptions of universal deity, Christendom derived its first impulse to monasticism from the same quarter and from the same Graeco-Egyptian god. If, in Milton's caustic phrase, "the ghost of a linen decency haunts us yet", the sacred use of linen, the surplice, is a last heirloom from the priests of Isis. But, as we shall see, Christendom had nobler gifts from Alexandria.

It is a very curious thing, however, to note how very

slight and casual are the references of any kind to Alexandria in the New Testament. Asia Minor is far more significant, doubtless a result of Paul being by birth a Cilician, and turning naturally to his own country and those adjoining it, which led to Europe. When Claudius Lysias asked Paul if he were an Egyptian, it is surely one of the strangest questions in the New Testament. A man whose name was half Greek, implying that he belonged to the eastern half of the Mediterranean, should have known an Egyptian when he saw one; he may have meant an Egyptian Greek or an Egyptian Jew; but he seemed surprised that Paul spoke Greek at all; and it is interesting to note that Paul repudiates the idea of Egyptian origin with the emphasis that we always find in him when he is strangely stirred. Why should it vex him?

In the third place, to recall what we have already discussed, the influence of Alexandria on Judaism is of the utmost importance. The synagogue was perhaps, in the first instance, developed in Babylonia, but it flourished in the Greek world, and in Alexandria. In the mad reign of Gaius, it was the happy freak of the heathen forcibly to convert the synagogues of Alexandria into temples of the Emperor. The Dispersion becomes typical almost in Alexandria, with the synagogue as its centre of idealism, nationalism, religion and literature, the place where on every seventh day, as Heine's poem tells us, the Jew was transformed from a dog to a fairy prince. For the Jews as for the Greeks Alexandria became the centre of a new literary activity. Here, if nowhere else, the idea of Alexander bore fruit; the Jew was effectively introduced to Greek thought and to Greek literature. The most outstanding result was the translation of the Hebrew scriptures into Greek—a novelty and a precedent with great results. Finally, though Judaism eventually discarded them, the writings of Philo, in which he attempts the reconciliation of Greek thought and Hebrew religion, have had an immense influence on Christian theology. What is more, life and letters in this place contributed to the development among the Greek-speaking Jews of a language of religion, which the early Church found ready to hand and of which it made signal use. It was a very great contribution indeed to the religious history of the world; for it has been well said that it was not until they found expression in Greek that the ideas of Jesus had a medium through which their greatness could be felt and recognized. That language of religion grew in the synagogues, the schools and the studies of Jewish Alexandria—once more a significant contribution to the history of the world.

Lastly, something must be said of the influence of Alexandria on the Christian world. In this city Jew and Greek in collision were working out a new language and new conceptions of religion, and in this atmosphere the new religion of the Gospel was preached with effect. Who first preached it, we do not know, but the work was momentous. The full force of Greek criticism was brought to bear upon the Christian message; it had to be thought out anew and related to all the best in the Greek heritage. It stood the test; and, toward the end of the second century, we find a great school in Alexandria of Christian philosophy, in which Greek thought, Greek letters and Greek culture are shown to be not incompatible with the following of Christ—no! proper to it, and inevitable. The Gospel captures new background, and a Christian philosophy begins to develop, as it must if Christ is to hold the reflective as well as the simple, if He is to be lord of all. Four great names must suffice here, true types of Alexandria. Pantaenus, the learned scholar who taught Clement, left Alexandria to preach Christ in India. India is a vague term; it might mean Abyssinia, it might mean anything eastern; but when Clement uses the term, and it is remembered that eighty ships in a summer would sail from the Red Sea port to the Malabar coast, it is probable that the India we know is meant. In any case the story is significant; in Alexandria the Christian becomes a philosopher, and the philosopher gives his life to carry out the idea of Alexander, that all the world is his parish, and that all that is good is to be held in common by all mankind—the idea of Alexander, and of Christ. The learned and charming Clement wrote the kind of book familiar in that day, woven of happy memories, bright allusions and pleasant thoughts. If now and then something fresh comes to him he is not hampered by an iron devotion to relevance; and he strays away, writing with a beauty, a gaiety and a style, that make the reader love him. Three quotations from the Gospel, and three from Greek literature perhaps in the same page, all to the glory of "my Orpheus, who sang to set the souls of men free"; so he pictures Christ. After him comes the still greater Origen, of the scholar type, an influence of the most significant in Christian thinking. Last of all, Athanasius, who made the imperishable contribution to the Christian church in insisting—Greek as he was— that there should be no compromise when men speak of Jesus Christ.

Whatever was in Alexander's mind, he did a great thing for mankind; the city and its thinkers and writers stand high in human history; and if we say, as we surely may, that Christ captured the strongest of them, what is the inference?

VIII

THE MAN OF THE EMPIRE

If the object proposed in the last chapter was difficult, the task before us surely will be impossible. How is anyone to generalize about the man of the Roman Empire? Draw a picture of the Englishman of to-day, and how many Englishmen will it fit? What picture will cover the features of the American people? The Roman Empire comprised many races, many types, and it was only Greek culture that unified them. Whatever is attempted here, it will be, as Aristotle says of his *Ethics*, broad outline rather than detail. Some points, already touched upon, may be recalled to round off our story.

Mr Tarn makes the suggestion that man as a political animal—the phrase is Aristotle's—had ended with Aristotle; with Alexander begins man as an individual.[1] There is more in the epigram than epigrams are often intended to give us. The political life has stopped, and man is confined to two aspects of reality, the universe at large and himself, both very difficult to realize or to understand. It is an interesting remark of Aristotle[2] (to which I shall have to come back at a later point[3]) that religion in any state is apt to follow fairly closely the form of the temporal government. Alexander abolished the "political animal", ended the significance of the *polis*, and made the

---

[1] W. W. Tarn, *Hellenistic Civilization*, p. 69.
[2] *Politics*, i, 2, 7, 1252 b.   [3] See p. 183.

temporal government monarchy pure and simple. Under his Successors, and perhaps even more under the Roman Empire, life becomes controlled, and consequently somewhat stereotyped. Towards this two great forces had been working. Democracy, as a Socialist pupil of mine once told me in an essay, "Democracy by its very nature leads to the apotheosis of the commonplace". How he reconciled this with his Socialism, for he was not commonplace himself, I did not ask. But it is too often true, as we can see, in the great triumphant democracies. The mass of mankind, instead of having its ideal set for it from above, is imposing its own ideals upon the exceptional man—insisting, in the dull, obscure, but definite and practical way of commonplace society, upon standardized opinions, conservatism in thought, orthodoxy in literature, and in religion and philosophy—when there is any of either—and, of course, in science which lends itself more easily to orthodoxy. If we try to reassure ourselves by thinking that the spread of education, as in England to-day to some extent, and in America more doubtfully, must have worked for the raising of standards, the standards were not rising very noticeably in the Hellenistic period; in some ways they are stereotyped, in other ways they degenerate. The idea of progress is a modern one, imperfectly thought out and ill-understood; it is not clear whether it is "automatic",[1] or whether, to be effective, it requires some consciousness of a goal; in the ancient world (apart from some Christian apologists, e.g. Tertullian and Prudentius) the very conception was missing. But,

1 We have learnt from Polybius to doubt this word; cf. p. 76.

broadly speaking, fourth-century democracy set the
conditions for the production of a standard manhood,
and under the control of an imperial authority from
Alexander onwards the race becomes more and more
incapable of producing anything but the average
person. Democracy and autocracy are re-inforced by
the philosophers. Plato's *Republic* is the dethronement
of the Athenian amateur and the enthronement of a
rigid system of authority. Men are to be brought up
so, and thus; and freedom of opinion is not to be part
of their education; travellers who may chance to go
abroad from the ideal community will be required on
their return to say that the institutions of the foreigners
are unequal to their own.[1] There were by the time
of Nero no foreigners left for comparison apart from
Parthians and barbarians. The criticism, passed by
Dr John Oman upon Plato and his *Republic*, is relevant
to our subject; viz. that Plato concerns himself mainly
with safeguards, Jesus wholly with venture. Control
is the mark of the Empire, no longer the gay freedom,
the lucky improvisation of Athens.

To these primary conditions this must be added.
Greece and, in various measure, Rome and Italy,
suffered from the sexes being on different levels of
culture—a very subtle danger which told on all life.
When woman is on a lower level of education than
man, she is more liable to be degraded socially and
physically; but she takes her revenge in paralysing—
as she can, as mother and wife—the intellectual development of the superior sex. And this is to be seen

[1] Plato, *Laws*, xii, 951. If Plato is not wholly serious on this point,
he is one of those writers who can play with what they believe.

in our period. The feminine conception of life is very well in women but not in men, even where woman at her highest sets the pace. But in this Empire woman was far from her highest, and, according to Dr Verrall, the disease, of which more than of anything else ancient civilization died, was an under-estimate of woman.

Turning, then, to the man of our Empire; let us begin with his education. One of the great sentences of the older Greece, always a pleasure to call to mind, is the vivid fragment of Simonides, πόλις ἄνδρα διδάσκει, "the city teaches the man"; but now there is no *polis* to teach the man. The city may be larger by far than any Simonides ever knew, cover more ground, have a street four miles long, and house more people; but it houses fewer ideas, and those it keeps are of less depth and intensity. The city is no longer a nation, a sovereign state; any patriotism it wakes is of a different order, antiquarian or commercial; there is no national passion in it; there is no international conflict of ideas or ambitions. The boy in the Roman Empire was no more educated by his city than the ordinary boy to-day by Stirling or New York. Renaissance Florence was another story. In America one of the subjects of the school curriculum is, or used to be, "Civics"; the boy was supposed to find, and the girl too, a certain training in the study of the city, its water supply, its sewage, and the control of the franchises of its streets. We can quite understand why in America it has been necessary to direct the attention of the young to problems of water and street planning, and to the value of the right to run tramlines over immense areas; the rights have been sold corruptly so often. But whether Civics is a desirable or effective means of education is another question, and the answer depends on our idea of the aims and nature of education. It is at least arguable that, if the training of the mind is our aim, we do better in our curious old country by letting our boys and girls learn Latin and Greek and forget the town council. A town council is not necessarily a thing of beauty or a joy for ever; and, such education as the study of its duties and procedure may give must be rather narrow. Education should be spiritual, and teach men to handle the eternal issues of beauty and justice, to take ever wider and wider views of mankind and of God. There was local government in abundance in the Hellenistic kingdoms and in the Roman Empire; but it seems rarely to have appealed to the better minds of the community. Yet a man, who, like Plutarch at Chaeronea, or T. H. Green at Oxford, will serve on such a body, gives his country an ideal. Still it is clear that city life could not be the broad education it once had been.

Let us turn to the more formal side of education, and look at the Greek boy at school. In the great old days of Greece there had been no system; there were hardly any schools worth talking about. Then the city educated the boy, with the aid of his father and a little help from his mother; the one text-book was Homer, who would be learnt by heart from end to end; and, somehow or other, Greece produced an amazingly brilliant type of man. Yet Plato did not like it, and in a passage of triumphant irony, he represents Anytos, the accuser of Socrates, maintaining stoutly that the average citizen is all the educator needed,[1] and, as usual with the opponent in Plato's dialogues, becoming wonderfully tangled in his talk. With the loss of empire and the decline of the city-state, Athens turned her mind to organizing education. Isocrates devised the intellectual side of it; others developed the ephebic system, which is essentially the cadet corps of the English public school. It is surely very suggestive for us that, when education was thought out, standardized and controlled, it produced nonentities with the utmost success. Why is the practice of culture so deadening? Why is it so difficult to combine intellectual stimulus, or even intellectual discipline, with a government department or an educational system?

"Rhetoric" was the comprehensive name for the new education. It included most of the things that a modern university rejects—the writing of essays, the development of thinking powers, the study of masterpieces of literature; and it has nothing to say about biology, or zoology, psychology, or any of the things which we reckon most important. Matthew Arnold once defined culture as "to be familiar with the best that has been said"—a great definition, like many of his definitions very suggestive, and very open to retort from people of less range and less independence than Matthew Arnold. Is it possible to be too familiar with the best that has been said; and, if so, what then? The immense strength of this old education, with its constant reference to the master minds of antiquity, the historians, the great poets and the great philosophers, and its intimate knowledge of their masterpieces, can

---

[1] Plato, *Meno*, 92 E.

be seen in the progressive hellenization of Christianity, as, still earlier, in the influence of Greek culture upon Judaism, which ended, as we saw, with the fall of Jerusalem and the rise of Christianity. The difference between the *Proverbs of Solomon*, so called, and the *Wisdom of Solomon*, gives some idea of the measure of it: and the contrast between a page of Clement of Alexandria and a page of St Mark tells the same story. But with all the immense impression that Greek education made upon the man of the empire, and, further, in spite of the real value of the education, it is too traditional: it knows only the approved standards of beauty and taste. "Who reads the Bible", says Tertullian, already a Christian, "who reads the Bible before he becomes a Christian?" St Augustine gives the reason; "it seemed to me unworthy of comparison with the dignity of Cicero".[1] The Latin Bible was written in a rough jargon, popular and illiterate; it lacked, in its literal renderings, as the Septuagint also lacks, the grace, strength and ease of Classical Greek and Classical Latin; and, because these things were missing, the educated would have none of it. In one case, however, as we saw, the great Longinus sees through the tawdry writing, and picks out one great example of the "sublime" in the books of Moses, who is "no commonplace person": "God said, Let there be light, and there was light". That is the great style, he says, the sublime. The collective judgment of mankind is for the classical masterpieces, and Aristotle[2] confirms this, urging that the judgment of the many

[1] Augustine, *Confessions*, iii, 5, 9.
[2] *Politics*, iii, 11.

169

in matters of taste and aesthetics is of more value than Plato would allow, who preferred an expert. That is worth remembering. The whole basis of education was literary and philosophical.

Aulus Gellius, in the reign of Antoninus Pius, composed his *Attic Nights*, a collection of notes or little essays on grammar, antiquities, history, biography, philosophy, legal points, textual and literary criticism, and other topics—"a hantle o' fine miscellaneous feeding", with references by name to two hundred and seventy-five authors. A man of moderate ability, but accurate and conscientious, with a strong leaning to old books and out-of-the-way learning, if he borrowed at times from other collectors, many of his day did the same. He won in different eras the praises of St Augustine and of Erasmus, both for his style and his learning, and to the leisurely student of our period he offers a pleasant picture of sympathetic culture, wide and genial if not profound. He is a typical Latin of the Empire.

There was criticism of the methods from time to time; Strabo[1] says that the grammarians put trifling legends before their pupils, and took pleasure in the ingenuity of language rather than in the solution of real questions. There are drawbacks, of course, about every university. "Mankind", Andrew Lang once said, "has been going to Oxford for some six hundred years, and is not yet perfect." The same sentence might have been applied to Athens, if anyone had had the wit and the courage to do it; certainly Synesius, in the fourth century A.D., would have hailed it with

[1] Strabo xiii, c. 616.

satisfaction as supporting his criticism of that ancient university. But whatever criticism be levelled at the standardization of taste and training, it was to a great literature that attention was directed and to a great history; and it is not yet established that the Greek standard of education, which prevailed in the days of Socrates 400 B.C. and still prevailed in the days of Dio Chrysostom A.D. 100, can be greatly improved upon. The great staple of education for a gentleman in the days of Socrates was an intimate knowledge of Homer; and as an education Homer takes a great deal of beating; even in the modern atmosphere of America, one translation of the *Odyssey* has had a sale, largely for schools, of 350,000 copies. "Let Homer", wrote Dio Chrysostom, "come first and middle and last for every boy and man and old man, to every man according to what he can receive. Lyrics, and elegiacs, iambics, dithyrambs, are admirable, if you have time . . . in tragedy Euripides, in comedy Menander; history is essential for a statesman, Herodotus for charm."[1]

In the First Book of Marcus Aurelius' Journal is a series of paragraphs of very great interest, in which he thanks his teachers one by one for what they have done for him: a practice not often observed in modern universities. This man and that man he thanks for the impression of their character. Here is one, whom he thanks for teaching him not to make a practice of saying "I am too busy". Another he thanks for teaching him to read "with his whole attention" until he accurately knows what he is reading, and not to be

[1] Dio Chrysostom, *Or.* 18, §§ 9, 6, 10.

content with a general impression. Another he thanks for "saving him from moral danger". Yet another, for "putting him on his guard against miracles"—the kind of miracle that was performed on streets. Other writers of his day speak of these magical performances, and Celsus contemptuously classes the miracles of the New Testament with them; only the vulgar would be taken in by tricks of the magicians as they called up the spirits of the dead, and presented the spectators with the sight of banquets which were not there; and so on.

But as a mirror of the culture of the early Empire there is no one comparable to Plutarch, of all authors after Herodotus the most genial, the most learned and the most human. He wrote easily and well on all sorts of topics, on history and religion by preference. He is more constructive than Gellius—longer in the staple; and he is not an orator like Dio. To this day his *Lives* are admirable reading, a pageant of interesting humanity, and in his *Moralia* we have the best that his age and school can offer in morals and religion. He has his limitations; he does not understand politics and he loves intellectual safety; but neither the age nor the training is to be lightly condemned of which he is typical. The passing of Plutarch out of modern education has not been pure gain.

Such were the main lines of education, and the literature follows them even too closely, until at the end of the second century we meet the two Africans, Tertullian and Apuleius, quite exceptional men, who knew all the artifices of the schools of rhetoric, and used them for purposes undreamed of by their teachers. But for the rest—

> Small profit have continual plodders ever won,
> Save base authority from others' books.

It was fashionable to write epics and to gather friends to a reception to hear them read by the author—"till the pillars cracked", Juvenal says. Happily we are not obliged to read them; time has seen to that. There was also that simple faith in the encyclopaedia that marks every age of halting culture —in handy guides to conversational knowledge. They wrote epigrams, very charmingly: they wrote acrostics; all sorts of things, all neat perhaps rather than great. But even when they were pleased with themselves, they realized that they were successors of men greater than themselves. *Magna illa ingenia cessere*, says Tacitus. The great geniuses had ceased to appear; but men were conscious still that behind them stood that amazing and glorious past.

When we pass within doors, there were in that ancient world perhaps as many varieties of household as in our own. That triumphant parody *The Banquet of Trimalchio* describes the household and the menu of an enormously rich freedman, but he was never supposed to be more than an excrescence upon society. Plutarch is more apt to take us into the ordinary home of the period than Petronius. Sir John Mahaffy[1] has pointed out that Plutarch also was in revolt against the wicked luxury of the day; and he invites attention to the extremes of luxury which provoked the protest: iced drinks—they were cooled, in fact, with snow—wether mutton, foie gras. It does not sound very wicked.

---

[1] J. P. Mahaffy, *Silver Age of the Greek World*, p. 386 n.

Pliny, in the same way, expresses that constant revolt of masculine sense against feminine luxury, which we find before him in Isaiah and after him in St Jerome, and which probably is invariably without effect. We have seen already Pliny's reference to silver and gold leaving the Roman Empire, a million sterling a year, exported to the Orient to fetch spices and silks—"so much our luxuries and our ladies cost us", he adds. Later on, he says, "all sorts and kinds of people wear silk, even quite vulgar people".[1] It is always a question, what is luxury: perhaps the best definition of luxury would be anything that is just a little more than one wants oneself.

Luxury, or at any rate, art, has spread into life, and the standard of taste advances. Suetonius, writing about A.D. 110, looks back over a century, and says that the furniture of the Emperor Augustus is scarcely fit for an ordinary gentleman's house to-day[2]—*pleraque vix privatae elegantiae*. The eruption of Vesuvius in A.D. 79, by burying Pompeii in mud, preserved for us the actual rooms in which the people of the town, or the better part of the town, lived. The rooms are very small, and the wall paintings are one of the great features. Thirty years ago it was remarked that out of some 3000 wall paintings which had been identified, three-quarters at any rate treated subjects from the mythology; and very pretty some of them are—though not all quite the thing for the domestic scene, some Victorians might have said. The loves of Jupiter make better art than theology; the watch dog on the *qui vive* in one picture, for instance, suggests Ovid rather than

[1] Pliny, *Nat. Hist.* xii, 84.   [2] Suetonius, *Augustus*, 72.

Zeno. Much of it has been brought to the Museum at Naples; and the French historian Grenier would have it that there were true artists even at Pompeii.[1] There is evidence of a passion for works of art; everyone must have them, copies of course; but cheap reproductions are perhaps not as fatal as some refined natures seem to suppose. Tertullian says idolatry was the midwife that brought us all into the world—all life and all art are steeped in idolatry. Money, of course, was spent on ornaments and jewels. A list of jewels hung on an image of Isis by a pious lady is very noteworthy; and it is probable that, if pious ladies hung jewels upon Isis, others less pious hung them on themselves. It is also clear that there was a weakness, surely a lovable weakness, for the collection of old furniture.

The houses were full of slaves, sometimes in enormous numbers—always a source of weakness and demoralization. The beauty of the Greek girl was too available for the moral atmosphere to be quite sound. A slave was liable to be a thief and a liar. In great houses it was too often with these people from the outlying parts of the world that the child grew up; and the Asiatic nurse might teach him (or her) all sorts of strange beliefs, as the negro nurse of the Southern States would do by her little white boys and girls. It was not the usual thing for the founders of Virginia and Georgia to carry a rabbit's foot in their pockets as a protection—a "hand" to safeguard them from "ha'nts". The papyri give an amazingly close picture of Greek life or Graeco-Egyptian life in Egypt, and

[1] Gaston Boissier's *Rome and Pompeii*, in an odd English translation, is delightful reading.

show us the people and all their little ways and daily affairs, including magic and charms. They let us into the secrets of families, and by telling us the names, as we saw in the last chapter, unfold the story of a mixture of races.

Toward the end of the second century a charming book called *Paedagogus* was written by Clement of Alexandria. It is a little book, treating, among other things, of good manners for Christians; and it seems to imply that some of them were rising in the world. Clement deals with health and manners and deportment. He recommends simplicity of diet, with health and strength as its objects. Those viands, to which the Gospels refer, such as fish and honeycomb, are admirable for such purposes. Boys and girls should not be given wine. Good manners commend the Christian; there must be no noisy gulping when he drinks, no spilling: he must not slobber his chin: he must not soil the couch on which he lies; and he will not hiccough. "How", says Clement, "do you think the Lord drank when he became man for us?" Vessels of silver and gold, furniture inlaid with ivory, rugs of purple and rich colours, are hardly necessary for the Christian, even if other people have them. The Lord ate from a cheap bowl, and washed his disciples' feet, with a towel round him. He did not bring a silver footbath from heaven to carry about with him. He asked the Samaritan woman to give him water in a vessel of clay. In general, Clement says, food, dress, furniture and all things of the house should be fitted for the person, his age and his pursuits. Man, again, he says, is a laughing animal, but he thinks that man should not laugh all the time. He recommends humour rather than wit or waggery, and, in an admirable sentence, he tells us the orderly relaxation of the face which preserves its harmony is a smile, not a giggle or a guffaw. In conversation low talk should be avoided. Man is a creature of peace, as the old greeting "Peace be with you" tells us. There are many other practices unfit for a Christian gentleman; and here he curiously approaches the author of a Book of Manners of the period of Charles II. The Christian gentleman should avoid spitting, coughing, scratching and other things. The little boy of King Charles' reign was not to spit indoors, unless in the corner of the room. The Christian should avoid whistling to the servants, or snapping his fingers to call them. Fidgeting is a mark of mental levity. Cleanliness, godliness and good manners are thus treated throughout with reference to the standards of the Lord. Plutarch also deals with manners, deprecating, like an American, the use of the left hand in eating. Dio commends to the Rhodians decorous bearing, tidiness of hair and beard, a sedate walk, becoming dress and a quiet manner.

The Macedonian had not originally locked his women up as the Greek did; a nation of peasants, unlike townspeople, needed woman's help out of doors; and the great freedom of the princesses of the Macedonian courts spread slowly down to the Greek home. Women entered chariots—probably they did not drive them themselves—at the races. They had clubs in some of the cities; and, positively, at Priene a woman, named Phile, was a magistrate.[1] Lydia at Philippi is

---

[1] W. W. Tarn, *Hellenistic Civilization*, 85, 86.

described as a dealer in purple, probably fabrics, and Phoebe of Cenchrea seems to have enjoyed some freedom of movement. Readers of Theocritus remember with joy those two homely good souls who go to the celebration in King Ptolemy's house—Gorgo and Praxinoe; there is very little about them that suggests antiquity or a foreign scene; but, as a modern writer has said, it is a wise dispensation of Nature to guard us against too great diversity in the character of races by providing that the women at least are essentially of one race.[1]

From the women to pass to the children, the exposure of infants still went on, and no doubt abortion too; but it is only too significant that the practice of infanticide, which to-day is the mark of the savage tribe, was one of the regular features of civilization. It was a constant feature of the plot in drama, and provoked the Christian rejoinder that we do not expose our infants and keep parrots instead. If one thinks of the consequences to the state and population, it may not have been really much worse than the modern habit of doing without a family; but taken in conjunction with slavery and gladiatorial shows, the frank brutality of the practice is evidence of a general outlook on life, which it must have helped to lower. Greek religion, it may be noted, did not forbid it; and one cannot help thinking that this very different sense of the value of the individual contributed to the victory of the Gospel, which proclaimed other standards of morality and tenderness learned from Christ. But we have also to consider this infanticide

[1] F. R. Earp, *The Way of the Greeks*, p. 51.

in relation to social and economic questions. Very often infanticide and its modern equivalent are evidence for economic conditions and social ambitions; and despair of the world may be another source of it. I came on a case recently of a Dutch family where the father refused to have children: he would not expose them to the horrible consequences of predestination— a curious reaction.

The interests of life, of course, were various. There was the garden, with the country house, which became more and more elaborate. Varro, in his book on country life, anticipates Cowper—

> God made the country, and man made the town.

"Divine nature made the fields, human art built the towns", Varro said.[1] Horace did not draw this distinction, but his poetry is full of references to Tibur. Simple pleasures meet us in our authors; the grave and old turn young again and gather shells on the seashore, and the boys send flat stones over the water, making "ducks and drakes".[2] There was travel. A wicked undergraduate once chose to misconstrue the line of Lucan describing the scene at Troy: *nullum est sine nomine saxum*. "Every stone has a name on it" was his rendering. It was not quite what the poet meant, and yet it is true of that ancient world. The tourist did write his name on the "antiquity" that he came to see. The oldest Greek inscriptions in the world consist of the names of Greek soldiers carved on the legs of

[1] Varro, *de Re Rustica*, iii, 1, 4, *divina natura dedit agros; ars humana aedificavit urbes*.

[2] See Cicero, *de Oratore*, ii, 22; and Minucius Felix, *Octavius*, 3, 5.

colossal statues of Egyptian kings: and the Roman did the same. He loved to travel. Sometimes he went abroad for the adventure, the sheer enjoyment of travel; no doubt fashion sent him to do the grand tour; sometimes his purpose was to be initiated into mysteries in various holy places. It is also very obviously an age of antiquaries, as the minute and careful *Description of Greece* written about A.D. 180 by Pausanias proves. The *Acts of the Apostles* gives a very vivid picture of the freedom of travel.

There are no politics; but there is always gossip, which a great thinker of my acquaintance pronounced to be a low form of communion of saints. The social life of Rome in the generation before Christ, as shown in Ovid and Horace, was brilliant enough in a superficial way, and if it seems rather lazy and selfish, what was to become of men, bred to politics and the clash of ideas, and condemned to inaction? Rome is repeating the experience of the Hellenistic world. Later on there is more sense of duty and more intellectual activity. No English gentleman could have more concern for the small but pleasant duties of the good citizen, for social graces and a certain attention to the mind, than the younger Pliny. One feature of the Empire in the day of St Paul, and for a century after, is the travelling lecturer, whose popularity implies a widespread feeling for the beauty of language (one sign of some degree of education) and whose lectures must have made some progress possible in the habit of reflexion (not too deep perhaps), in the study of the great literature, and emphasis on conduct. Dio Chrysostom is a master of pleasant phrase, easy thought, kindly feeling and also of moral discipline. In the fifth century his admirer Synesius tells us (and he admits it himself) that in his youth he was like the peacock, always turning round to admire the spread of his tail, but there came a change; and, instead of making orations for display, Dio now in simpler and directer words preached sermons, or something very like sermons, on the care of the moral life. He was one of the few thinkers of antiquity who had a word to say about the moral claims of the prostitute to be considered and treated as human, and not abandoned to a barren Aphrodite—a fine development. Aelius Aristides is another of these harshly named rhetoricians, to whom we owe some very interesting speeches about the faith cures of Aesculapius. He tells us how once he was suffering abominably from toothache; everybody else in the temple had gone to some entertainment in the great theatre which still stands in Epidaurus; the god told him to make a speech to cure his toothache: he obeyed and delivered a speech in the empty temple, to the sacristan; and his toothache was miraculously healed.

The philosophy of that age still holds mankind. The Stoic Epictetus can still be read with admiration, though the four books of his discourses, which Arrian, the historian of Alexander and the "Xenophon" of those times, took down as he spoke them, have a certain suggestion of monotony, as any four books of moral teaching might. There is besides the Diary, or rather Journal, of Marcus Aurelius which again indicates the power of Stoicism. It is a strange and rather unhappy book, the Breviary (it has been called) of

Agnosticism. Everything except his duty is an open question for the great Emperor, a soul as solitary as his throne and his philosophy could make a man—"even in a palace life may be lived well". His book too has a certain monotony, if read consecutively. To do the book and the Emperor justice, it must be read in snatches, as it was written. Grim as they are, Epictetus and Marcus remind us that the age still produced nobler natures, and they also reveal how little Stoicism was in any sense a religion.

Apart from philosophy there was something of science. Eratosthenes was still studied. Strabo writes his *Geography*, which no scholar can use without gratitude and enjoyment. Seneca and Plutarch compiled volumes of scientific questions. The criticism is on the whole fair, that they are more apt to see the failure of the explanations they have received than to engage in any research which will produce the true reason or confirm the facts to be explained. Galen's name reminds us that medicine still produced thinkers, and to him we owe the epigram about the type of people who give absurd reasons for facts which do not exist. Seneca has no scientific vocabulary, which may not have been an absolute disaster; but he has a very remarkable faith in the future of science. He predicts a growing knowledge, and a time when the interpretation of the mysteries of nature will be more familiar to everybody. It belongs, perhaps, to this part of our subject, to ask whether astrology is a science. We find, at any rate in the West, more evidence than ever before of serious attention being given to it, while, in the East, Bardaisan wrote in Syriac a discussion of the relation between the stars and destiny. The subject is discussed again in his *Confessions* by Augustine who had to use reason and observation to rid his mind of its influence. It is a strange fact, that, whether it is astrological or scientific, it is in this first century A.D. that the planetary week was adopted, with a suddenness quite unexplained, in our western world, and spread outside the Roman Empire well ahead of Christianity, as the German names, and our own names, for the days of the week prove; they are neither Christian nor Latin, but they preserve the planetary week. The Roman world, in its idleness, betrayed a curious craving for the occult, the mystical, the oriental. Horace bids Leuconoe not meddle with "Babylonian numbers"—horoscopes, in plain words—but take life as it comes. But the Chaldaean was able to vend his art in strata of society that never read the poet. Lucian's *Lover of Lies* reads like parody till one is familiar with what was talked and believed.

George Finlay notes the growing separation of higher and lower ranks, the lower, he says, without philosophy and the higher without religion. The impulse, which Alexander, in uniting the world into one empire, had given both to religion and philosophy to seek a universal unity, was not spent. Universal goddesses, and later a universal god in Mithras, begin to overshadow local cults; and religious thinkers move toward an accommodation between one god and many—the latter local manifestations of the one, or emanations from him. The dominant idea of the times is syncretism—the amalgamation of all the religions that mankind has known into a system. It is given a very philosophic look and flavour at last; but it rests on unexamined assumption—certain questions, Plutarch's father said, were not to be asked, because they upset religion. The key to the popularity and to the weakness of Neo-Platonism is that it accepted the popular gods, as Plutarch did his physical facts, without examination, and then accounted for them by a magnificent and all-embracing theory, with nobler elements borrowed from Plato. The plain fact was that philosophy declined and made terms with superstition. Men had begun to be afraid of life, had "lost nerve", and for safety tried to hold at once every available belief. There was a very great deal of superstition, and the thinkers for two centuries preach against it—Cicero, Horace, Plutarch (with reservations), and the scoffers deride it; but in vain. Magic, in the absence of science, holds the field. The ancients knew little of double pneumonia and appendicitis, and any sudden death, which we might explain by these diseases, they would put down to magic. They may have had more grounds than we to credit tales of poisoning.

The "mysteries" are talked about to-day out of all proportion to their significance. On the other hand, no man can read Seneca and Epictetus without being impressed with the sense and dignity of their moral teaching. Mr Rand in his *Founders of the Middle Ages* gives a remarkable list of quotations: moral sentences of force and insight, not from the Old Testament or the New, but from the classics. The conception of monotheism was as familiar to cultivated minds in Greece and Rome as in Judaea. Indeed, I would go so far, and be so provocative, as to say, that, if the

Jesus of certain scholars is the true one, the peasant dreamer with his head full of Apocalyptic and the clouds, living in an imaginary world, I think we should do better to read Epictetus: he is at least sane and strong. But the historian of religion is bound to ask why mankind moved over to Christ, and why the monotheism of the cultivated mind was so powerless to produce the conviction and character which the apologists magnificently, and justly, bid us recognize in Christian slaves and slave-girls. Through the thinking and religion of the day, pagan and Christian, runs the influence of Plato taken as an authoritative teacher rather than as a philosopher. The strength of Platonism can be seen in Clement of Alexandria and Origen, as in the Neo-Platonist movement of the third century.

The three main features of religious thinking in this age may be summed up as follows. First, we have the strong thought-out morality of the Stoics, resting on nature and conscience ($\phi\acute{v}\sigma\iota\varsigma$ and $\sigma\upsilon\nu\epsilon\acute{\iota}\delta\eta\sigma\iota\varsigma$)—a robust philosophy still valid for the facts on which it is based. Its weakness was that it ignored too much in human nature, that it isolated man and kept out God (allowing Him honorary rank of course in the universe), that it put too heavy a load on the individual and struck at personality.

In the second place, we have mysticism revolting against Stoicism on these very grounds, and offering the weak and the solitary the promise of a ready communion and identification with traditional and wholly unexamined gods by means so simple as holy food, holy abstinence and holy words. Adherents of intuition may defend them, but it is not a contemporary defence in any wide degree; and the cults palliated too much that was indecent and immoral.

Thirdly, we have sheer uneasiness manifested in all kinds of superstition and in all kinds of eclecticism.

There is, no doubt, a great deal that is right and admirable in Neo-Platonism, as in the Stoicism and Scepticism that it drove out of the field. But, as the great German scholar has said in reply to those who maintain that all that is of value in Jesus' teaching is to be found in the Talmud: "Yes! and how much else". A great deal of the morality of this period is admirable, but somehow or other there is lacking the dynamic which will set men free from what is not so admirable.

But there is further evidence as to the religious mind of the day in the writings of the Christian apologists which were addressed to the thinking public. They had a strong sense of responsibility to the people with whom they dealt, and a real desire to meet their difficulties, and the criticisms they brought against the new religion. Their appeal is uniformly and strongly to the reason, the justice, and the moral sense of an educated and fair-minded society. Five points may be noted.

They always have to deal with the question of authority. The pagan is thoroughly in subjection to the Emperor, the magistrate, the civil servant and the law. The law has laid this or that down, and there is no getting past it. To this Tertullian rejoins, "An unjust law has no authority". He anticipates that appeal to "a higher law" made by the abolitionists in the United States before the Civil War, an appeal that never fails to irritate the strict constitutionalist. This ascendancy of law gives a real clue to the mind of the day.

Secondly, the apologists are always confronted with the antiquity of the old religion: and they take two lines, showing that there was a great deal of uncertainty about the history of the old religion, and at the same time using the Old Testament to get an ancient background for the new faith—using it with a mixture of literalism and allegory that is appalling till one realizes that they owed their method to Philo and the Stoics.

Thirdly comes culture; Christians have no culture, no education. Celsus sneers at the new religion: the faith of the fuller and the baker—the stuff that the slaves talk in the corner of the verandah to the mistress and the children, when the master is away, and always to the keynote of "only believe". It is only necessary to read a page of Clement, with its beauty, and its intimate knowledge and enjoyment of the Classics, to see that there was as much culture on the Christian side as on the pagan, and a great deal less contempt for men and women whom man had robbed of culture and freedom and everything, but for whom Christ had died, and in whom He had believed as being capacious of God to the fullest. So much for defence.

When it comes to the offensive, our fourth point is the emphasis laid on the futility of the old religion driven home with passion and reason. If, as Euhemerus taught, the gods were once men—"What a pity", says Tertullian, "that they did not deify better men while they were about it!" If, on the other hand, they are spiritual beings, then explain, says the apologist, why they are expelled by the ordinary Christian every day in the name of Jesus: they cannot stand against the new faith. Further still, he carries the war into the enemies' country by insisting upon the very dubious morals of the gods and of their rites. And the same thing is true of India to this day. The Government of India in forbidding the exhibition of obscene symbols, the use of obscene language, has to exempt the temples from the operation of the Act. This was a feature in the religion of the ancient world, and the desperate defence made by Plutarch emphasizes the weakness at which the Christian strikes. And again, the old religion is really and essentially inconsistent with the best philosophy of the old world itself. This was true; and it is driven home relentlessly by a battery of quotation from the whole field of ancient philosophy, which is quite surprising in a community of bakers and fullers, and surely illustrates our contention that Christianity actually did touch the better minds at their best.

Above all, they emphasize the moral regeneration of the new faith—the change of character, the honesty, the purity, the courage, that marked whole classes of the community which the ancient world despised. Women and slaves, clothed with a new power, rival Socrates himself in the gladness and the courage with which they die for the new faith, and live in a new spirit. Mr Earp points out that there is no Greek word for "unselfishness". Quite apart from that and the negative words in which we have too often expressed the virtues, Paul's epistle to the Galatians gives us a whole series of positive words representing positive virtues which the Stoics did not know—love, joy, peace, gentleness, goodness, faith. But, more than anything else, it was the death of the martyr in the arena which shook the candid spirit of that ancient world; and that in itself is evidence that we are dealing with a real race of men who are doing real things.

Here I end, for the present; and it seems to me that, if what I have tried to set out in these chapters answers to the evidence (and I think it does), then it surely results, first, that the Church came into being in a world with great features and great needs and a great inheritance, and that it conquered the world because it appealed to a great race on its highest levels. And, if the story I have told is a true one, it invites to a fresh study of the power of the Gospel.

BOOKS

THE following list contains the names of a number of books, chiefly English books, written on the basis of high scholarship but in such a spirit and style as to bring out the human values of the subjects treated and to appeal to any reader who is interested in ideas and movements.

Chapter II, *The Greek.*

Sir R. W. LIVINGSTONE, *The Greek Genius and its Meaning to us.* Oxford University Press, 1912.

A. E. ZIMMERN, *The Greek Commonwealth*, fourth edition. Oxford University Press, 1924.

The Legacy of Greece, edited by Sir R. W. LIVINGSTONE. Oxford University Press, 1921.

GUSTAVE GLOTZ, *Ancient Greece at Work*, English translation. London: Kegan Paul, 1926.

JAMES ADAM, *The Religious Teachers of Greece*. Edinburgh: T. & T. Clark, 1908.

Chapter III, *Alexander.*

D. G. HOGARTH, *Philip and Alexander*. London: John Murray, 1897.

W. W. TARN, *Hellenistic Civilization*, second edition. London: Edward Arnold, 1929.

(Mr Tarn's chapters on Alexander and the Hellenistic Age in the *Cambridge Ancient History* should be read)

Sir JOHN P. MAHAFFY, *Greek Life and Thought from the age of Alexander to the Roman Conquest*. London: Macmillan & Co., 1887.

EDWYN BEVAN, *The House of Seleucus*. London: Edward Arnold, 1902.

EDWYN BEVAN, *The Ptolemaic Dynasty* (vol. IV of *A History of Egypt*). London: Methuen & Co., 1927.

Chapter IV, *The Roman.*

ALBERT GRENIER, *The Roman Spirit*, English translation. London: Kegan Paul, 1926.

BOOKS

W. WARDE FOWLER, *Social Life at Rome in the Age of Cicero*. London: Macmillan & Co., 1908.

GASTON BOISSIER, *Cicero and his Friends*, English translation, sixth edition. London: Ward, Lock & Co. (no date).

Chapter V, *The Jew*.

ALFRED BERTHOLET, *A History of Hebrew Civilization*, English translation. London: G. G. Harrap & Co., 1926.

W. O. E. OESTERLEY and T. H. ROBINSON, *Hebrew Religion, Its Origin and Development*. London: S.P.C.K., 1930.

W. FAIRWEATHER, *The Background of the Gospels*. Edinburgh: T. & T. Clark, 1908.

Chapter VI, *The Roman Empire*.

GASTON BOISSIER, *Roman Africa*, English translation. London: G. P. Putnam's Sons, 1899.

M. P. CHARLESWORTH, *Trade Routes of the Roman Empire*, second edition. Cambridge University Press, 1926.

C. A. J. SKEEL, *Travel in the First Century*. Cambridge University Press, 1901.

F. HAVERFIELD and G. MACDONALD, *The Roman Occupation of Britain*. Oxford University Press, 1924.

H. F. TOZER, *A History of Ancient Geography*. Cambridge University Press, 1897.

Chapter VII, *The Hellenistic Town*.

F. HAVERFIELD, *Ancient Town Planning*. Oxford University Press, 1913.

Chapter VIII, *The Man of the Empire*.

Sir SAMUEL DILL, *Roman Society from Nero to Marcus Aurelius*. London: Macmillan & Co., 1904.

H. M. GWATKIN, *Early Church History*. London: Macmillan & Co., 1909.

CONSTANT MARTHA, *Les Moralistes sous l'empire Romain*, cinquième édition. Paris: Hachette et Cie., 1886.

PRINTED
BY

WALTER LEWIS, M.A.

AT
THE CAMBRIDGE
UNIVERSITY
PRESS